PANINI

PANINI

carlo middione

PHOTOGRAPHY BY ED ANDERSON

TEN SPEED PRESS
Berkeley | Toronto

Ten Speed Press
PO Box 7123
Berkeley, California 94707
www.tenspeed.com

Distributed in Australia by Simon and Schuster
Australia, in Canada by Ten Speed Press Canada,
in New Zealand by Southern Publishers Group,
in South Africa by Real Books, and in the United
Kingdom and Europe by Publishers Group UK.

Cover and text design by Toni Tajima
Food and prop styling by Jenny Martin-Wong

Library of Congress Cataloging-in-Publication
Data
Middione, Carlo.
Panini / Carlo Middione ; photography by Ed
    Anderson.
        p. cm.
Summary: "A collection of fifty recipes for
    traditional and modern-day panini (Italian
    sandwiches)"—Provided by publisher.
Includes index.
ISBN-13: 978-1-58008-895-4
ISBN-10: 1-58008-895-3
1. Panini. 2. Cookery, Italian. I. Title.
TX818.M54 2008
641.5945—dc22
                    2007039774

Printed in Singapore
First printing, 2008

1 2 3 4 5 6 7 8 9 10 — 12 11 10 09 08

CONTENTS

PREFACE

Many kindred panini lovers have helped and encouraged me in my panini perambulations. On many road trips and around countless tables, favored companions have been not only family and friends but also panini partners. My wife, Lisa, is always at the top of my list of helpers—and in many more ways than just being my panini partner. Nothing good I do, or could do, could be done without her. Among many friends and peer eaters who have given advice, and recipes, and panini themselves, Anna Tasca Lanza and Nancy Harmon Jenkins stood out in their enthusiasm for this book and shared their favorite panini eaten over many miles of road and at the table.

I thank Lorena Jones of Ten Speed Press for letting me write down many delicious panini recipes. Thanks also goes to my editor, Brie Mazurek; Ed Anderson, our photographer; Jenny Martin-Wong, our food stylist; and Toni Tajima, our designer.

So many others have provided me with information that made it easier, and certainly fun and rewarding, for me to write down the recipes, and to you all, many, many thanks. And *buon appetito*!

INTRODUCTION

"Charming company turn lowly sandwich into rich banquet."
—*Charlie Chan in Reno* (1939)

SINCE TIME IMMEMORIAL, there have been sandwiches; they simply were not called that. A piece of meat folded over a blade of grass or a shoot, a root, or a nut, an edible leaf containing a grub or tiny raw fish, and *ecco*, you have what we call a sandwich. In time, as food became more complex to prepare and quite diverse, thanks to socialization, agriculture, and the never-ending quest for "what's new" in taste, more ingredients were at hand to try. Not all experiments are planned, or follow protocol set by others that eventually leads to a conclusion—a theory that gets proved. No. When it comes to sandwiches, or in our case panini, you will see that it must have been happenstance that created a nourishing, and novel, way to eat more than one item at a time that is, at the same moment, the ultimate portable feast.

You can put a panino in your pocket and set off to see the world, never having to worry about hunger, or brave the wilds to bag game, or plow the fields to generate crops. Ever since Rabbi Hillel, the great Jewish teacher who lived about one hundred years before Christ, put haroseth (a delicious concoction of fruit and nuts) between pieces of matzo, sandwiches have been abundant but strangely neglected in literature and certainly in most cookery books from all ages. Here, we correct that.

Most often credited with first putting some meat between two pieces of bread is the great gambler John Montagu, fourth earl of Sandwich, in the mid-eighteenth century. It was said that he created this portable snack to satisfy his hunger while he gambled, so he wouldn't have to leave the thrill of the game. From primordial times to John Montagu to panini is circuitous to be sure, and not in the scope of this book.

TRAMEZZINI

In Mussolini's time, before World War II, panini were seen as too pedestrian for a great nation to munch on, so they were banned as such. Of course, enterprising Italians came up with a new word, *tramezzini* (in-between things), and a daintier look. These are outrageously popular in bars and *osterie* in Italy, accompanied by the inevitable glass of wine, or maybe a coffee or dense hot chocolate. They are a little like what we call tea sandwiches, just slightly bigger.

A MOVEABLE FEAST

This book is about making and eating panini—Italian-style sandwiches. Who but the Italians eat with such exuberance and have such a love of ingredients (and are so fussy and determined about getting the best of them)? Who but the Italians cook with such a sense of adventure that they have raised a simple meal like a sandwich into an edible art form?

In Italy, there must be tens of thousands of panini variations. Many of them probably originated as a slice or chunk of bread eaten alternately with a bit of something else, most probably semi-hard cheese, but also other things such as cured meat, dried fish, or fruit. Cheese travels well or sits deliciously on a table with nothing to conserve it but the salt it contains, getting flavor and character from milk and the loving skilled hands of the cheesemaker. The same is essentially true of cured meats.

From Roman times, meals of bread accompanied by bits of cheese and meat for flavor were called *companatico*, from the Latin *cum panis*, "with bread." The word *companion* has the same root, sharing, in this case, to go with bread. In Italy still, olives, prosciutto, cheeses, and salted fish are known as *companatico* ingredients. "*Voglio comprare un po' di companatico.*" "I want to buy a little something to go with bread." Usually these ingredients are salty or highly flavored because bread, even in its most robust form, benefits from more assertive partners. Today, we enjoy these traditional panini fillings, but also more contemporary ones like roasted vegetables, freshly cooked or canned fish, even fruit, chocolate, and ice cream!

At some point, the need arose for food that was portable. Or, when one had more bread than filling on hand, someone eventually thought to put both to good use by capturing small amounts of filling between two pieces of bread. And so panini were born. As the sandwich became more popular, of course a type of bread evolved just for it. The Italian word for bread is *pane*. A small bread or roll is *panino*. More than one roll is *panini*. The rest you can imagine.

PANINI EXPLAINED

If you think panini are closed, invariably grilled sandwiches, you will be amazed by the variety, as revealed in this book. The term *panino*, as I'm using it, is the generic name for sandwich in Italian. There are some sandwiches in this book that are open-faced, some that are not grilled, and some on unlikely styles of bread. The idea that panini must be grilled and pressed is strictly American. In Italy, not all panini are grilled, and many would suffer if you did grill them. There, grilled panini are especially popular in fall and winter, and when you need to be comforted. But in the height of summer, a non-grilled tomato and mozzarella panino might be the choice of many eaters.

With Italian panini, tastes are pretty much dictated by what one has on hand and what is locally produced and available. Because the variety of tastes is as diverse as the regions of Italy, ingredients go from chicken liver to roasted vegetables to simply cheese and a bit of prosciutto. As noted before, panini as Americans perceive them are relatively new to Italians. Italians have become quite adventurous by making panini out of ingredients that were normally served as a *contorno*, or side dish.

I selected the panini to include in this book because, first and foremost, they are delicious. They celebrate diverse tastes, textures, and outstanding ingredients such as prosciutto, speck, anchovies, buffalo milk cheese, and so on. These panini show some novel and delicious ways these ingredients can be used—as the Italians use them. The variety of panini is literally endless if you have a sense for the combination of flavors. Even if you don't live near the best-stocked Italian goods market, you can, with a little sleuthing, find almost any ingredient needed.

Authentic Roadside Panini (*Panini dell'Autostrada*)

What Americans would call "gas stations" are found along every major Italian *autostrada* (highway). But gas stations, Italian style, have full-scale restaurants, some of which serve food so good it is hard to believe. Panini are a major favorite on these routes. They can be bought quickly and eaten just as quickly, either while driving or during a rest stop at the station. When I eat one, I feel like I just survived a hair-raising trip on the Amalfi coast with two wheels of the car almost off the side of the so-called road that is really a cliff with the sea hundreds of feet below!

Of the many virtues of *autostrada* panini, I consider two as best: they are fast and easy to make and they are authentic, with no need of embellishment. They tend to be austere by American standards: simple, delicious ciabatta-style buns moderately filled with mortadella, salami, prosciutto, prosciutto *cotto* (cooked ham)—that's it!

Do not let the seeming austerity throw you off. Good bread and good meats or cheese will satisfy you, and you will taste flavors as never before because they are not masked with the usual suspects such as mayonnaise (good as it is), mustard, pickles, lettuce, tomato, and so forth. You eat them as they are, for the quality and taste of the bread, and for the outstanding cured meats found all over Italy, from far north to far south. Young people and children are particularly drawn to the simple, yet elegant direct tastes of authentic *autostrada* panini.

SALUMI (ITALIAN COLD CUTS)

Pancetta: Often mistakenly called Italian bacon, pancetta is made just like prosciutto, not smoked. A slab of pork belly is salted and rubbed with regional herbs, rolled into a very thick log resembling a jelly roll, and left to cure for at least three months. If sliced thinly, it is similar to prosciutto, only a bit chewier.

Prosciutto: Prosciutto is the highly salted rear thigh (ham) of the pig. It must be air-cured and dried for at least fourteen months to be considered any good at all, and it's often better if cured longer.

Mortadella: This is a contraction of the names for how it was made: *mortaio della carne* (a mortar used to pound the meat) was over time condensed to *mortadella*. Mortadella is finely pounded or ground pork mixed with spices and usually pistachio nuts and black peppercorns.

Salami: This describes a whole range of large, spicy dried sausages, usually made of pork but sometimes beef. Salami is usually dried at least six weeks, or up to several months. It is best eaten sliced very thinly.

Soppressata: A typical southern Italian salami that has chunks of pork meat (as opposed to ground meat) seasoned with black peppercorns. In general, it is smoother and tastes more of meat and less of the heavy spices than salami.

Speck: Speck starts out being the same cut as bacon: pork belly. It is salted and cured for a number of weeks and sometimes months. It is then lightly smoked to give a distinctive woodsy flavor.

CHEESES

Asiago: This semi-firm cow's milk cheese is from the Veneto region. It has a nutty and rich flavor that makes it ideal for panini.

Fontina: Real Italian Valdostana cow's milk cheese is rich and creamy. It has a pale yellow color and tastes slightly nutty.

Goat cheese: Fresh, young goat cheese is great for use in panini. Its flavor can be sharp and lemony and is delicious with fresh berries or dried fruit.

Gorgonzola: This blue-veined cow's milk cheese is pungent, rich, and creamy. It is delicious with salami or prosciutto.

Mascarpone: This high-fat, smooth, silky cow's milk cheese is often eaten like a pudding. It marries well with berries or with salty cured meat.

Mozzarella: There are two types for the most part: fresh buffalo milk mozzarella, which is soft, tender, and very mild; and the firmer cow's milk mozzarella.

Provolone: A firm cow's milk cheese, provolone is aged about three months and has a natural flavor that is slightly smoky.

Ricotta: Ricotta literally means "recooked." When whey from other cheeses is heated, ricotta floats to the top. It is smooth and moist.

Pecorino: The two most famous styles are Pecorino Romano, which most of us know simply as "Romano," and Pecorino Sardo, very similar to Romano but from Sardinia and richer in flavor. Pecorino fresco, which is fresh, semi-firm sheep's milk cheese, is nutty-sweet.

Taleggio: From Lombardy, this semi-soft cheese is pungent and nutty, pale yellow and sometimes a bit smelly.

Modern Panini (*Panini Moderni*)

Modern panini were born out of city life and pace, and, of course, the incredible ethnic diversity of urban populations. The panini in this chapter are to be enjoyed both for their deliciousness and for their sense of adventure. More and more, families are eating panini in place of pizza or a traditional dinner with two or more courses. The ease of making panini and the relaxed dining atmosphere they inspire promotes this kind of a meal to a growing audience.

First to love modern panini were the *paninari*, young Milanese hipsters of the 1980s who wore outlandish outfits—like boldly striped socks, garish wool hats, madly decorated denim vests—and who hung out at the *paninoteca*, the "sandwich library," where a large variety of panini are sold. *Paninoteche* are still very popular all over Italy. They are fun, and the panini concocted by the *paninoteche* owners are outstandingly good.

Autostrada panini created a category of eating not found in traditional meal courses: they were a fast, delicious, handheld mini-meal. In time, the word *panino*, which originally meant a little roll, came to also mean sandwich. Now when you shop in Italy you have to make quite clear what you want: bread or sandwich.

As panini grew in popularity, panini makers started using more daring ingredients, such as caviar, speck, and seared tuna. Thus, we have what I call modern panini, and the recipes in this chapter are only the beginning.

Sweet Panini (*Panini Dolci*)

In the sweet panini chapter, I present panini that fare equally well as desserts or mid-morning and afternoon snacks, with cooked and fresh fruit, chocolate, cheeses, even gelato. These panini are made for Italian street life but are perfectly at home *in* the home. They are fun, tasty, and easy to make—and everybody loves them.

ABOUT BREADS

Throughout this book I've offered suggestions as to which bread I think works best with the ingredients in the recipe. Of course, you will use what you think is best and what you like.

Generally speaking, a panino—little roll—should be a soft bread, but not mushy or wet by any means. It must be chewy and very slightly elastic: sturdy enough to cradle the other ingredients, but tender enough that you can take a bite and gently pull away a mouthful of delicious flavors. A true country bread with a heavy crust that shatters when cut or bitten is ideal for open-faced panini like bruschetta, the famous wood-fire-toasted bread rubbed with whole garlic and anointed with the best quality extra virgin olive oil. Probably the most popular kind of bread for panini is ciabatta. Use either the elongated "slipper"-shaped bread loaves or individual rolls. Where I live, they are readily available, and I eat a lot of them! You'll find a recipe for ciabatta on page 16.

Other breads to enjoy as panini and available here include whole wheat; hardtack (a rigid bread round made of whole wheat flour mixed with a small amount of rye flour, a specialty of Alto Adige, the Italian- and German-speaking northern region); focaccia, mostly used in the southern part of Italy; and the dense, crumbly bread from around Ferrara called *coppia*.

For more substantial panini, I prefer rolls, which make a bigger sandwich. For generous, but sensibly sized panini, I like loaf bread. Choose either a crusty type for "rustic" fillings such as grilled vegetables, or a thin-crusted Pullman style (Italian *pane in cassetta* or French *pain de mie*—both baked in a pan, rather than free-form) for less assertive ingredients. If you use a Pullman bread, try to get one with some whole wheat flour added. Not only is it more flavorful, it also has a better texture, and toasts very well.

For ciabatta rolls, simply cut them lengthwise into tops and bottoms. For ciabatta or other rustic, flat loaves, cut them crosswise into sections that are about $3^1/_2$ to 4 inches wide, then halve them lengthwise into tops and bottoms. You'll get a very nice amount of bread that accommodates almost all the panini in this book.

Of course, there are many other ways to slice a loaf of bread. You may choose to cut a ciabatta loaf, which is quite flat and makes smaller panini, crosswise in sharp diagonals, which produces long, slender slices. With very large country breads that yield large slices, you might consider cutting the panini into quarters or thirds for ease of eating.

EQUIPMENT

Here are some of the typical, reasonably priced tools you can use to make panini. Most are available at well-stocked hardware, department, and kitchen equipment stores. I have made panini on every appliance described below with good results and tasty eating.

Electric Panini Grill

When calling for grilling or toasting panini, I have used an electric panini grill in most, if not all, of the recipes, because I assume you will already own one. If you don't, you should consider buying one. Electric panini grills are handy, easy-to-use machines that do the job well. They are also versatile because they can be used to make more than panini. They make excellent toast and can cook certain meats, fish, and poultry. Most of them have removable grates or plates that can be washed.

When shopping for a grill, look for a heavy-weight, expandable hinge, so that the upper plate can accommodate thick foods such as bulky sandwiches; easy-to-clean outer surfaces to prevent grease buildup; and most important, the highest wattage possible. High wattage not only makes for a faster heat-up time, but it also helps grill ingredients more evenly and quickly.

Stovetop Grill

I love my stovetop grill and use it often. It can grill panini as well as vegetables, meat, fish, and fowl, with or without a weight on top. To grill panini on both sides, it is nice to have a moderate weight applied while grilling. I use a heavy skillet, a flat dinner plate weighted with a couple of cans of tomatoes on top, or any flat-bottomed object that weighs about 2 pounds. A garden brick wrapped in aluminum foil will work, too.

A stovetop grill is convenient because it is flat and low and can be easily stored. I've found that a small one that covers a single burner works better than the kind that straddles two burners because there is a space between the burners that simply does not get hot enough. The small stovetop grill is nice for one or two items, but its size is also its disadvantage. The two-burner one holds much more, even though the heat can by spotty.

Griddle Pan

I also like to use a griddle pan to make panini. Usually made of cast iron but sometimes aluminum, it looks like an iron skillet but has deep ridges on the bottom. It works like a stovetop grill and is in fact one in itself. I find it handy and easily maneuverable on the burner.

Waffle Iron

A waffle iron is usually considered a single-purpose cooking utensil. I love waffles, but when I want an open-faced panino that can hold lots of flavor, I use the waffle iron to grill thick slices of Italian bread. The resulting pockets make for an unexpected presentation and are perfect for holding flavorful goodies like extra virgin olive oil, chopped olives, bits of cheese, red pepper flakes—you name it. Most waffle irons are electric, but some older models can be used over gas or propane flames. These are fun to use and with practice give excellent results.

Skillet

Even if you don't want to purchase special equipment, don't despair: you don't need any of the previously mentioned equipment to make excellent panini. A good old skillet (of which you probably already own several) will do nicely.

For grilling panini, choose a skillet that is big enough to hold them without crowding. Place it over medium heat for about 2 minutes to get it warm. Butter or oil one side of your slices of bread, assemble your panini with the oiled side out, and place them on the warm skillet. Place a plate with a couple of tomato cans sitting on top (or another flat surface with a 1- or 2-pound weight) atop your panini. After about 2 minutes check to see if the bread color is as you like (usually a nice golden color) and make sure the panini ingredients are getting hot. If not, raise the heat slightly. When done, turn the panini over, and repeat the process on the other side.

MAKING PANINI

Panini can be as unique as the individual who makes them. This may seem like license to do anything, but free expression has a price. It must come from a point of view and with some kind of discipline, some kind of grounding, and at least a nod to what came before—to tradition. Some of the panini in this book are, indeed, classics, with no need for change; in fact, it would be a pity to change them. They are delicious proof that not everything is improved by reinvention, that what is good is good and must be respected as such. But you should also have fun and make up panini as you go. Who knows, you might well come up with a new classic yourself.

I hope you make panini a part of your life for the rest of your life. I hope the Italian in you prevails when you search out the best, most flavorful breads and the best ingredients to pair with them. Panini are great companions—there we go again, *cum panis*! Share these good and tasty offerings with your family and your friends, and use them to welcome strangers into your camp as well.

CONTORNO

When eating panini, good as they are on their own, sometimes they are even better with a *contorno*, literally, "contour"—something that either contrasts with or reinforces the taste and texture of a dish. In many of the recipes, I've suggested such an accompaniment, which can be anything from a few olives to cut-up raw vegetables to salads to dried fruit. For instance, to add crunch to a panino of goat cheese and salami, the *contorno* is thinly sliced bulb fennel, zucchini, and bell pepper. To emphasize the sweetness of a panino of prosciutto and melon I've called for a *contorno* of dried figs and dates. These are *my* favorite accompaniments. Let them inspire you to devise your own *contorno* to suit your tastes.

BASIC RECIPES

ricette di base

CIABATTA CIABATTA

makes 2 (1-pound) loaves or 8 (4-ounce) rolls

Ciabatta ("slipper" bread), which originated at Lake Como, is probably the most popular Italian bread one finds in local bakeries these days. Ciabatta is delicious simply toasted. I love it for panini or just general good eating.

A warm proofing area where the dough can properly ferment makes all the difference, as does an oven that maintains a steady, even heat.

Like most European-style country breads, this one uses a simple-to-make starter that needs to age 8 hours to overnight. It's easiest to mix it the night before your bread-baking session. The starter improves the flavor and texture of the bread, giving it depth and character.

Note that Italian 00 flour is softer than American all-purpose, and certainly much softer than our bread flour. If you want bread more like that found in Italy, use unbleached all-purpose flour and mix it with 25 percent pastry flour or cake flour. This will approximate the Italian flour. However, you will still have a very nice bread if you use only American all-purpose flour.

STARTER

$^1/_8$ teaspoon active dry yeast

$^3/_4$ cup warm water (110°F or less)

$1^1/_4$ cups all-purpose flour

To make the starter: In a heavy bowl, combine the yeast and 2 tablespoons of the warm water to soften the yeast. Add the rest of the water and the flour. Mix thoroughly with a large spoon or a heavy spatula, and loosely cover with a plate or lid askew. Let rest at room temperature for at least 8 hours; overnight is better. It must be very alive and bubbly.

DOUGH

1³/₄ cups all-purpose flour, plus additional for dusting

1³/₄ teaspoons sea salt

Extra virgin olive oil

³/₄ cup warm water (110°F or less)

To make the dough: In the bowl of a heavy-duty mixer fitted with the paddle attachment, combine the 1³/₄ cups flour, salt, and yeast and mix well at medium speed. Add all of the starter and the ³/₄ cup water, and mix until all just holds together in a sticky ball. It will be hard to handle; add additional water if needed. Continue to mix on medium speed for about 3 minutes, or until it begins to smooth out and is no longer *terribly* sticky. Change to the dough hook and knead for another 4 minutes, until the dough is still sticky but springing back on itself.

On a flat work surface (a baking sheet with sides is good), spread plenty of flour in a wide circle and turn out the dough onto the floured area. Pat the dough all over the top with some olive oil, and dust with a thin veil of flour. Cover with lightly oiled plastic wrap and let rest in a warm spot (about 75 to 80°F) for about 30 minutes. By using a baking sheet you can move it around to warm spots in the kitchen as needed. The dough should start to bubble a little. Using a dough scraper, a large metal spatula, or your hands greased with olive oil, pick up one edge of the dough, stretching it a little, and flip it over onto the center; repeat

continued

with the other side. Let it rest another $1^1/_2$ hours, flipping the dough in the same way twice more, about every 30 minutes or so.

Preheat the oven to 450°F for at least 30 minutes, having a heavy baking sheet or a pizza stone big enough to hold 2 loaves in the oven during this time to also preheat. Set the sheet or stone on the middle rack of the oven. While the pan preheats, form the loaves. With a dough scraper or large metal spatula, cut the dough in half and roughly shape each half into the classic slipper form: a rounded rectangle about 16 inches long and about 5 inches wide. Use your well-greased or floured hands to gently stretch the dough. Cut 2 pieces of parchment paper, each a little bigger than 1 loaf, and flour them generously. Flip each loaf onto a piece of floured paper. Cover with oiled plastic wrap, oiled side down, and let proof in a warm spot about 30 minutes. The loaves should almost double in size. Uncover and dust the tops of the loaves liberally with more flour. Dimple the tops of the loaves with your fingers, making little craters all over, but don't deflate the dough.

To bake the bread, slip a baker's peel or wide, flat spatula that completely supports the loaf under each loaf, one at a time, and slide the loaves onto the preheated sheet.

Bake for about 30 minutes, or until the bread has a very dark, almost chestnut-colored crust. Mist the oven with water 2 or 3 times in the beginning of the bake to help develop a good crust, and rotate the loaves around the oven once, for even baking. If you like a darker, stronger crust, bake a total of about 40 minutes, or longer.

Cool the bread on racks with plenty of air circulation to achieve a nice crunchy crust. Let cool completely.

SIMPLE BREAD DOUGH PASTA PER PANE SEMPLICE

makes 1 (1-pound) loaf or 4 (4-ounce) rolls

This is a slightly simpler bread recipe, though it still takes several hours. You can double or triple the recipe with no problem.

1   cup warm water (about 110°F)

1½ teaspoons fresh or active dry yeast

¾ teaspoon sea salt

2   cups all-purpose flour

Put the warm water in the bowl of an electric mixer. Crumble the fresh yeast into the water or sprinkle the dry yeast over the surface. Let rest for about 5 minutes. The yeast should begin to bubble up and show it is alive and working. Add the salt and flour.

Attach the dough hook, and start the mixer on low. Knead until the dough becomes a cohesive mass that slightly sticks to the sides of the mixing bowl, about 4 minutes. Liberally flour a work surface and transfer the dough to the floured surface. Knead by hand for about 2 minutes, to give it shape. Put the dough into a lightly oiled bowl; use the mixer bowl if you like. Cover with plastic wrap and let the dough rise in a warm (75 to 80°F) place in your kitchen for about 2 hours, or until doubled in volume. Punch it down with a clenched fist, cover again, and let rise for another hour or so, until doubled in volume. The bread's texture is best when proofed twice, but if time is an issue, you can have a decent loaf with only one proofing.

continued

Remove the dough from the bowl and shape it as you like. For panini, the best shape is long and narrow, about 16 inches long and 3 or 4 inches wide. For panini rolls, cut the dough into 4 pieces and shape them round or square, as you like. Lay the bread on a floured surface and cover with lightly oiled plastic wrap. Proof until doubled in volume, about 45 minutes.

Preheat the oven to 450°F about 30 minutes before baking time, setting a baking sheet or pizza stone on the middle rack to preheat as well. To get a "bakery look" you could sprinkle a *light* veil of flour on top of the loaf just before putting it into the oven. You can bake the loaves as is, or make a $1/4$-inch-deep slash lengthwise or three $1/4$-inch-deep diagonal slashes; they aren't necessary but help control the rise of the loaf as it bakes. The rolls need no slashes.

Put the bread into the oven on the preheated baking sheet or pizza stone. Slide a large spatula under the bread. (If you do not have one, use a heavy, solid piece of cardboard cut bigger than the bread, and dust it liberally with flour.) You could also proof the bread on a floured baking sheet and simply put it into the oven.

Bake the bread for about 10 minutes, misting the oven once with water in a spray bottle, or place $1/2$ cup water in a low-sided pan and set it in the oven anywhere it fits. Lower the temperature to 400°F and bake for about 25 more minutes (15 minutes, if making rolls), or until the loaf is deep gold. To test for doneness, remove the loaf with heavy kitchen mitts or towels and knock the bottom crust with your knuckles. If it sounds hollow, it's done. If it makes a dull thud, bake for 5 to 10 minutes longer. Let cool completely on a rack to allow circulation all around the loaf; it could get soggy in spots where there is no air.

MIXED GREEN SALAD INSALATA DI VERDURE serves 4

This adaptation of my mother's salad is an all-around favorite of mine that pairs really well with most of the panini in this book. In the spring, if you can find ramps, a delicious type of wild onion, substitute them for the red onion.

1 head of Bibb or other butter lettuce, as yellow and tender as possible

1/2 head of frisée (baby chicory), young and tender

1 pint small vine-ripened tomatoes, or 3 medium tomatoes

1 small red onion, thinly sliced

4 Persian cucumbers or 1 large English cucumber (unpeeled), quartered lengthwise and cut into 1/2-inch-thick slices

6 to 8 tablespoons extra virgin olive oil

2 tablespoons red wine vinegar

1 small clove garlic, minced

1/2 teaspoon sea salt

1/4 teaspoon freshly ground black pepper

1/2 teaspoon dried oregano

To prepare the salad, separate the lettuce and frisée into leaves and wash the leaves. Dry them thoroughly, until they are totally free of any moisture. Halve the tomatoes if they are small, or if large, core and cut into 6 or 8 wedges. Toss the lettuce, frisée, tomatoes, onion, and cucumbers in a large bowl.

To make the vinaigrette, combine the olive oil, vinegar, garlic, salt, pepper, and oregano in a bowl and vigorously whisk to blend thoroughly. Drizzle all over the salad. Toss quickly and thoroughly and serve.

"LITTLE" SALAD OF TURNIPS AND CUCUMBERS
INSALATINA DI RAPE E CETRIOLI serves 4

In northern Italy, vegetables like turnips and cucumbers are abundant. While turnips are often cooked, they are occasionally eaten raw, as in this salad. Letting the *insalatina* sit for at least 2 hours (up to overnight, covered, in the refrigerator) makes it even better and smooths out its tartness a bit.

2   medium turnips, peeled

³/₄ English cucumber

1   teaspoon white wine vinegar

Pinch of freshly ground white pepper

Halve the turnips, then cut crosswise into thin slices about ¹/₈ inch thick, or cut into ¹/₂-inch dice. Cut the cucumber the same way (do not peel). Toss both vegetables in a bowl with the vinegar and the white pepper to make a kind of zesty salad.

BASIC VINAIGRETTE VINAIGRETTE DI BASE
makes about 1¹/₃ cups

Here's a simple vinaigrette, great for use on salads. The ratio of oil to vinegar is always 3 to 1. For lemon vinaigrette, simply replace the vinegar with lemon juice.

1   cup extra virgin olive oil

¹/₃ cup white wine vinegar or freshly squeezed lemon juice

1   teaspoon sea salt

Freshly ground black pepper

In a small bowl, mix the olive oil with the lemon juice, then add the salt and good pinch of pepper; whisk well.

PESTO PESTO makes about 1 cup

The famous pesto alla Genovese usually uses pine nuts, but pesto with walnuts is a variation I like to use.

2 cups tightly packed fresh basil leaves (about 2 bunches, stemmed)

2 large cloves garlic

3 tablespoons untoasted pine nuts or walnuts

2/3 cup finest-quality extra virgin olive oil, plus more for topping

5 tablespoons freshly grated Parmigiano-Reggiano cheese

2 tablespoons freshly grated Pecorino Romano or Sardo cheese

1/2 teaspoon sea salt (optional)

Put the basil leaves in the jar of a blender or work bowl of a food processor fitted with the metal blade and pulse 3 or 4 times, until the leaves are chopped and compacted a bit. Do not overmix or the basil will heat and turn black and may even begin to ferment soon after it is made into pesto.

Add the garlic and nuts to the basil and blend until almost a paste. Do not overmix and heat the pesto. Add the olive oil and run the machine until you have a somewhat loose paste. Stop the machine, add the cheeses, and pulse several times more, until you have an unctuous, glistening green mass (the ingredients should be finely chopped but identifiable). Taste the pesto, and leave as is if it is salty enough from the cheeses; otherwise, adjust with salt to your taste. Use the pesto immediately or store it until needed in a clean, carefully washed and dried glass jar with a tight-fitting lid. Carefully float about 1/8 inch (a little more is better) of extra virgin olive oil on top, tightly secure the lid, and refrigerate (do not freeze) for up to 6 months.

AUTHENTIC ROADSIDE PANINI

panini dell'autostrada

MORTADELLA AND PROSCIUTTO DI PARMA
PANINI PANINI CON MORTADELLA E PROSCIUTTO DI PARMA serves 4

I have eaten dozens of these on my many road trips throughout Italy. Each time they seem to taste better and better; simplicity combined with superior ingredients makes a perfect meal on the go. To ensure the best-quality mortadella and prosciutto, buy them from knowledgeable staff at well-established Italian delicatessens.

CONTORNO: Radishes, yellow and tender celery stalks from the hearts, and whole green onions, drizzled with a little olive oil and sprinkled with sea salt and freshly ground pepper, if you wish.

Unsalted butter, slightly softened, for spreading

4 ciabatta rolls, halved lengthwise, or 1 (16-ounce) ciabatta loaf, cut crosswise into quarters, then halved lengthwise

4 ounces mortadella, thinly sliced

4 ounces prosciutto, thinly sliced

Spread a thin layer of butter on both cut sides of the rolls and layer an equal amount of the mortadella and prosciutto on the bottom halves. Cover with the roll tops, gently pat closed, and cut each panino in half for convenient eating.

These are also very good toasted in a panini grill. Do not butter the outside of the bread. Simply toast the assembled panini on a preheated grill for about 5 minutes on each side, or on a ridged stovetop grill about 4 minutes on each side, turning once (see page 11). Serve immediately.

"OPEN" RICOTTA CHEESE PANINI

PANINI DI RICOTTA APERTI serves 4

High-quality ricotta will taste naturally "sweet." I like that, and do not use any salt. Try it, and add salt if your taste requires it. Either a cool dry white wine or a moderately dry red is good with these *panini aperti*. This open-faced sandwich uses one of the pieces of toasted bread per serving, so a single bun will make 2 servings.

CONTORNO: Thinly sliced red onion and capers.

12 ounces whole-milk ricotta cheese

1 teaspoon dried oregano

½ teaspoon coarsely ground black pepper

2 ciabatta rolls, halved lengthwise, or 4 ³/₄-inch-thick slices wholewheat country bread

¼ teaspoon red pepper flakes, for sprinkling

Sea salt

Preheat a panini grill to high. Meanwhile, put the ricotta, oregano, and black pepper in a bowl and combine gently and thoroughly, folding rather than mixing. Don't mash down the ricotta—keep it fluffy.

Toast the bread to make nice golden stripes here and there, so it's crunchy on the surface with a soft crumb. While warm, spread each piece with a thick layer of the ricotta mixture. Sprinkle with the red pepper flakes and salt to taste. Cut each piece of bread in two for ease of eating, if you wish. Serve slightly warm.

GOAT CHEESE AND SOPPRESSATA SALAMI
PANINI PANINI DI FORMAGGIO DI CAPRA E SOPPRESSATA serves 4

These are assertive but smooth and satisfying panini. The lemony and tangy flavor of goat cheese and the smooth and peppery taste of the soppressata are brought together with the slightly smoky provolone. The butter provides a bit of coolness of taste and amplifies the texture of the other ingredients.

CONTORNO: Thinly sliced bulb fennel, zucchini sticks, sliced red onion, and bell pepper sticks.

Unsalted butter, at room temperature, for spreading

4 ciabatta rolls, halved lengthwise, or 1 (16-ounce) ciabatta or country bread loaf, cut crosswise into quarters, then halved lengthwise

4 ounces soft goat cheese

4 ounces provolone cheese, thinly sliced

4 ounces soppressata, very thinly sliced

Spread a thin layer of butter on both cut sides of the rolls. Spread the goat cheese evenly on the bottom halves, followed by a layer each of provolone and soppressata. Cover with the roll tops, gently pat closed, and cut each panino in half for convenient eating.

RYE HARDTACK WITH SOUTH TYROLEAN
SPECK PANE DURO DI SEGALE ALLO SPECK serves 4

With its crunchy, yet tender texture, this bread is addictive. But if you prefer, you can substitute soft, commercially packaged or artisan bakery rye bread for the hardtack. The combination of unsalted butter countered by the mild smoke of the speck (cured, lightly smoked pork belly) makes these little bits ideal to serve with a cold wine from northern Italy, such as Pinot Bianco. These panini are also delicious served with beer or a fruity white wine. Spoon a crunchy vegetable salad alongside the hardtack on each plate—a perfect accompaniment.

CONTORNO: "Little" Salad of Turnips and Cucumbers (page 22).

2   large (10-inch-diameter) rounds rye hardtack (about 6 ounces)

Unsalted butter, at room temperature, for spreading

½   small white onion, very thinly sliced

6   ounces speck, thinly sliced

1   ounce shredded fresh or jarred horseradish

Break the hardtack by snapping off pieces with your hands or by gently tapping the rounds with a hammer or similar tool. Generously butter the pieces of bread and scatter on a nice amount of the white onion. Top with 2 layers of speck, cutting the meat to size if necessary. Finish with a bit of horseradish. You will have several pieces of bread per person, depending on how the hardtack broke. Arrange attractively on plates and serve with some of the salad.

MODERN
PANINI

panini moderni

PAPA'S STEAK PANINI

PANINI DI BISTECCA DELLO PAPÀ serves 4

As a young apprentice to my father, a trained Italian chef, I often shared simple meals with him—just the two of us. When the panini are pressed, the cooking juices are absorbed into the bread. Instead of making the bread soggy, the juices make the bread cling to the meat. When sliced, the panini hold together very well, making them easy to eat. We used our trusty sausage press to make them, but a bookbinder's press or large duck press also works. These panini remain among my very favorites—easy to make, delicious, and memorable. We always had them with a big, bold, dry red wine.

I like to serve the panini in the parchment paper they are pressed in. It is casual and festive, and to me it replicates the "Papà panini" (that's what I called them) that I shared with my father. Waxed paper will work, too.

CONTORNO: Thinly sliced raw bulb fennel, thinly sliced white onion, and Belgian endive leaves.

---

1 to 1½ **pounds best-quality top round steak (about 1 inch thick), trimmed, at room temperature**

Sea salt and freshly ground black pepper

¼ **cup extra virgin olive oil**

½ **cup dry Marsala**

1 **(16-ounce) ciabatta loaf, cut crosswise into quarters, then halved lengthwise**

Season the meat with plenty of salt and pepper, and let it rest at room temperature, loosely covered, for about 30 minutes.

Have a warmed heavy plate ready. To cook the meat, in a large, heavy skillet (I use an old, well-seasoned cast-iron one), heat 2 tablespoons of the oil over medium heat. Brown the steak for 2 minutes on each side, or until slightly crusty, being careful not to overcook it. Remove from the heat. Add the Marsala, and turn the steak a few times to anoint it well with the wine. Transfer the steak from the pan (reserving the pan juices in the skillet) to the warm plate and let it sit for about 10 minutes (it should be medium-rare to almost rare). To test for doneness, cut the steak with a small sharp knife and pry open the slit. If it looks very pink, it is done. Juices will collect in the plate.

To prepare the panini, brush the remaining olive oil on the cut surfaces of the bread; dip all 8 bread pieces, cut sides down, into the juices left in the skillet. Transfer the bread, juiced side *up*, to a large plate and drizzle with the other juices collected from the resting meat. Divide the meat into 4 equal pieces and put each on a bread bottom. Cover with the remaining bread sections and gently push down. The bread should be very moist, but not soggy. Tightly wrap each panino in parchment paper to seal well. Put as many panini as will fit into a press, and apply pressure (about 2 pounds should do it). Leave it in the press for about 10 minutes. You can do this in batches if you have only a small press. Keep the pressed, wrapped panini warm in a low oven until you are ready to eat them.

When you are ready to serve, unwrap the panini (save the parchment paper for serving) and cut each one into 4 long mini-panini. Present on plates lined with the reserved parchment paper.

GRILLED CAPRI-STYLE MOZZARELLA PANINI

PANINI CAPRESE ALLA GRIGLIA serves 4

I made these panini once in a great rush. They were so well received that I now make them "on purpose" all the time. Try to use Sicilian dried oregano—the flavor is smoother and the fragrance more intoxicating than regular oregano.

CONTORNO: Gaeta or kalamata olives (though the latter can be very salty).

1 large ball fresh mozzarella cheese (about 8 ounces)

4 ciabatta rolls, halved lengthwise, or 1 (16-ounce) ciabatta loaf, cut crosswise into quarters, then halved lengthwise

1/4 cup extra virgin olive oil

2 medium firm, ripe tomatoes, cored and cut into 1/4-inch-thick slices

Salt and freshly ground black pepper

2 teaspoons dried oregano

About 12 fresh basil leaves, for layering

Slice the mozzarella and let drain on folded paper towels. Preheat a panini grill to high. Place the bread, cut side down, on the grill and toast quickly to mark with golden stripes here and there. Remove the bread from the heat and drizzle generously with olive oil.

To assemble the panini, put the tomato slices on the bottom halves of the rolls. Season with salt, pepper, a sprinkling of oregano, and a drizzle of olive oil. Arrange the mozzarella on top of the tomatoes. Season again with salt, pepper, oregano, and olive oil. Top each piece of bread with 2 or 3 whole basil leaves. Cover with the roll tops. Gently push down to compress slightly. If you want the cheese a little melted, assemble the panini as described and put them in a moderately hot panini grill for 8 to 10 minutes. The bread should toast nicely and melt the cheese a bit. Cut each panino in half for convenient eating.

ARTICHOKE AND TUNA PANINI

PANINI DI CARCIOFI E TONNO serves 4

If you keep a jar of good-quality artichokes packed in extra virgin olive oil on hand, a plus a few cans of choice Italian tuna, you will have panini to enjoy on a moment's notice.

CONTORNO: Mixed greens dressed with olive oil (from the can of tuna), sea salt, and freshly squeezed lemon juice.

4   ciabatta rolls, halved lengthwise, or 1 (16-ounce) ciabatta loaf, cut crosswise into quarters, then halved lengthwise

2   (6-ounce) cans imported Italian tuna packed in olive oil

1   (7-ounce) jar oil-packed roasted artichokes, drained and coarsely chopped

1/3 cup finely chopped green onions (white and pale green parts), or 1/4 cup finely chopped red onion

2   fresh basil leaves, coarsely chopped

Freshly ground black pepper

Juice of 1 lemon

Pull out some bread from each roll half, not much, to form a kind of basket; set the rolls aside. Drain the tuna but not completely (the oil is good and quite tasty). In a large bowl, combine the tuna, artichokes, green onions, and basil. Mix all together just to combine—it should be chunky. Add plenty of black pepper and the lemon juice, and mix again.

Divide the tuna mixture among the roll bottoms, cover with the roll tops, and press gently to close. Enjoy them cold or grill on a panini grill on moderately high heat for about 6 minutes, or until the bread has golden grill marks. Serve the panini quartered or halved.

ITALIAN-STYLE GRILLED CHEESE PANINI
"TOAST" ALLA FONTINA VALDOSTANA serves 4

Many Italians call grilled cheese sandwiches "toast." Often a thin slice or two of prosciutto is added, as in this recipe. I prefer fontina cheese, which is almost always used in Italy, but Asiago fresco and Taleggio are also very good.

CONTORNO: Capers and green olives mixed with extra virgin olive oil and oregano.

Unsalted butter, at room temperature, for spreading

8 ½-inch-thick slices white Pullman sandwich bread (pain de mie or pane in cassetta)

3 or 4 ounces Fontina Valdostana, Asiago fresco, or Taleggio cheese, thinly sliced and cut to fit the bread

Freshly ground black pepper

8 thin slices prosciutto di Parma or San Daniele

Butter 1 side of the bread slices, and arrange the fontina on the buttered side of 4 of the slices. (You can butter both sides, if you like.) Dust liberally with pepper. Lay 2 slices of prosciutto on the fontina. Cover with the remaining 4 slices of bread, buttered side down.

For best results, preheat a panini grill to moderately hot and brown the sandwiches on the grill. Toast the panini until the cheese melts and the bread is marked with golden stripes, about 10 minutes. Alternatively, use a stovetop grill: Preheat the grill to moderately hot; arrange the panini in the pan and cover with a 1- or 2-pound weight. Toast, turning once, until the cheese melts and both sides of the bread are golden brown and marked with stripes by the grill, 6 to 8 minutes. Cut each panino in half for convenient eating.

AMERICAN-STYLE "BLT" WITH PANCETTA
PANINI ALL'USO AMERICANO COME "BLT" serves 4

A classic BLT—bacon, lettuce, tomato—is at the top of the American sandwich list. Here it is made with pancetta, also from the belly of the pig like bacon, but milder and tastier than bacon, and not smoked. Equally select are the condiments: tender butter lettuce, heirloom tomatoes, and silken mayonnaise supercharged with extra virgin olive oil. I also love these goodies with beer.

CONTORNO: Green olives or pepperoncini.

16 slices pancetta (about ⅛ inch thick)

4 ciabatta rolls, halved lengthwise

¼ cup mayonnaise

1 tablespoon extra virgin olive oil

Coarsely ground black pepper

1 small head of Bibb or other butter lettuce, separated into leaves

2 large, ripe heirloom or beefsteak tomatoes, cut into ¼-inch-thick slices

Cook the pancetta until golden brown on a panini grill on medium heat or in a heavy skillet over medium heat, turning once. Drain on paper towels and set aside. (The pancetta can be browned up to 1 day ahead and refrigerated. Reheat under a broiler or in a panini grill.)

Preheat a panini grill to high. Place the bread, cut side down, on the grill and toast quickly to mark with golden stripes. Mix the mayonnaise with the olive oil and spread on the bottom halves of the rolls. Arrange 4 slices of pancetta on each roll so that all the bread is covered. Sprinkle with pepper. Top each with 2 large lettuce leaves and 2 or more slices of tomato. Cover with the tops of the rolls, gently pat closed, and cut each panino in half for convenient eating.

SAUSAGE, BELL PEPPER, AND ALMOND PANINI
PANINI DI SALSICCIA E PEPERONI ALLA MANDORLATA
serves 4

These panini require the best and freshest Italian sausages you can find, like Sicilian fennel. I make my own, but many high-quality Italian delicatessens sell respectable sausage. With a simple green salad, this makes a terrific lunch or a nice picnic. Serve with a slightly fruity wine.

CONTORNO: Mixed Green Salad (page 21).

2   tablespoons extra virgin olive oil

2   large red or yellow bell peppers, cored and cut into 1/2-inch-thick slices

2   large cloves garlic, thinly sliced

1   tablespoon toasted slivered almonds

1   tablespoon currants or small raisins

1   tablespoon red wine vinegar

1   pound uncooked Italian sausage links

Sea salt and freshly ground black pepper

4   ciabatta rolls, halved lengthwise

To prepare the filling, in a large, heavy skillet, heat the olive oil over medium heat. Add the bell peppers and sauté until the peppers soften a bit and have nice little burnt spots on them here and there, 4 to 5 minutes. Transfer the peppers to a plate and reserve. Add the sliced garlic to the skillet and sauté until pale gold, about 1 minute. Remove the skillet from the heat, add the peppers, and mix gently. Add the almonds, currants, and vinegar and stir well again. Put the skillet back on the heat for about 3 minutes, stirring the mixture vigorously. Remove the mixture from the pan and put it into a bowl for later. This mixture can be made a day ahead and kept refrigerated, tightly covered. Gently reheat it in a skillet when ready to serve.

continued

To roast the sausage, preheat the oven to 375°F. Put the links in an ovenproof pan and roast until dark gold, about 25 minutes. Prick with a fork; if the juice runs clear they should be done. Let cool for about 5 minutes and slice or coarsely chop. Set aside and keep warm.

To assemble the panini, preheat a panini grill to high and toast the bread on one or both sides, as you like, to mark with golden stripes. Halve the sausages lengthwise. Spoon a big mound of the bell pepper mixture on the bottom halves of the rolls, and add 2 sausage halves. Cover with the roll tops and gently pat closed. Cut each panino in half for convenient eating and serve warm.

CHICKEN LIVER PANINI

PANINI DI FEGATINI DI POLLO serves 4

Chicken livers are popular almost everywhere in Italy. In Tuscany, one of the most popular dishes is *fegatini*, which are chicken livers often made with the expensive, rare, and fabulous vin santo, and served on plain crostini. Make the livers as directed here to mix into pasta or to spoon on polenta, and save some for tasty cold panini treats a day or two later. For panini, either cold or hot chicken livers are equally good. White or red wine or whiskey are nice choices to serve with the panini.

CONTORNO: Arugula leaves, sliced radishes, and cut pieces of orange, dressed with extra virgin olive oil, some lemon juice, sea salt, and freshly ground black pepper.

$1/2$ to $3/4$ cup extra virgin olive oil

1 medium onion, finely diced

2 cloves garlic, finely chopped

12 dried juniper berries

About 7 large fresh sage leaves, coarsely chopped

12 ounces chicken livers, coarsely chopped

$1/3$ cup dry red wine

Sea salt

4 ciabatta rolls, halved lengthwise

In a large, heavy, shallow skillet, heat 2 or 3 tablespoons of the olive oil over medium heat. Sauté the onion, stirring often, until soft and slightly golden, about 7 minutes. Add another tablespoon of oil if the skillet looks dry. Add the garlic and sauté another few minutes. Add the juniper berries, sage, and chicken livers. Stir well, and cook about 4 minutes, until the livers are slightly rare. Add the red wine and salt to taste and cook about 5 minutes more. Remove from the heat and mash lightly with a fork. The livers should

continued

be very moist, fairly pink, and slightly chunky—don't make a puree of them. If they are too dry, add some more wine and cook a few minutes longer to eliminate the alcohol.

Preheat a panini grill to high. Toast the rolls quickly to mark with golden stripes. Slather the remaining olive oil on the bottom halves of the rolls (you may have a bit of olive oil left over). Spoon on a nice thick layer of chicken livers, cover with the roll tops, and gently pat closed. Cut each panino in half for convenient eating.

CHICKEN BREAST AND SUN-DRIED TOMATO PANINI PANINI DI PETTO DI POLLO E POMODORI ESSICATI serves 4

In general, I prefer chicken thigh meat, but if you must eat breast meat, these are great panini; tasty, colorful, and perfect for picnics. You can prepare the ingredients ahead and assemble the panini just when you want to serve them.

CONTORNO: Thinly sliced cucumber and red onion, or "Little" Salad of Turnips and Cucumbers (page 22).

1/3 cup extra virgin olive oil

Sea salt and freshly ground black pepper

2 teaspoons chopped fresh sage leaves

1/2 teaspoon red pepper flakes

4 (6-ounce) boneless chicken breasts, with skin or skinless

1/2 cup sun-dried tomatoes

4 ciabatta rolls, halved lengthwise, or 1 (16-ounce) ciabatta loaf, cut crosswise into quarters, then halved lengthwise

12 large fresh basil leaves, for layering

To make the marinade, combine 2 or 3 tablespoons of the olive oil, salt, pepper, the chopped sage, and the red pepper flakes in a small bowl. Place the chicken in a self-sealing plastic bag, pour in the marinade, and seal the bag. Turn a few times to coat the chicken, and let marinate in the refrigerator at least 2 hours or overnight, turning once.

If the sun-dried tomatoes are oil packed, use them as is. If they are dried, soak in 2 cups boiling water for about 4 minutes, drain, and pat dry. Chop the tomatoes up medium-fine.

Preheat a panini grill to medium, and grill the chicken until it is done and nicely golden on the surface, about 12 minutes. Set aside and keep warm. Wipe the grill clean. Lightly grill the bread, and brush a little bit of the olive oil on the cut sides. Cut the chicken breast into thirds on a sharp diagonal. Place 1 cut-up breast and some sun-dried tomatoes on each of the roll bottoms. Tear the basil into large pieces with your fingers, and distribute it over the tomatoes. Cover with the roll tops and gently press closed. Cut each panino in half for convenient eating.

ALMOST CLASSIC ROMAN EGG-DIPPED PANINI WITH CHEESE

MOZZARELLA IN CARROZZA QUASI CLASSICO serves 4

I must have eaten at least a hundred of these on my Roman journeys. Mozzarella *in carrozza* ("in a carriage") is usually deep fried, but sometimes it is oven-roasted. Use real *mozzarella di bufala*, if possible, because it is made from real buffalo milk and is the best tasting mozzarella there is.

CONTORNO: A dozen anchovy fillets, drizzled with lemon juice and seasoned with coarsely ground black pepper; and whole romaine lettuce leaves served with in olio santo (extra virgin olive oil laced with lots of red pepper flakes) for dipping.

8 ounces fresh mozzarella cheese, thinly sliced

8 slices Pullman-type sandwich bread (pain de mie or pane in cassetta), crusts removed

1¹/₂ cups whole milk

2 large eggs

¹/₂ teaspoon sea salt

¹/₄ teaspoon freshly ground black pepper

Extra virgin olive oil, for brushing the panini grill

Divide the cheese equally among 4 of the bread slices. Top with the remaining slices of bread and gently press closed. Halve each panino with a sharp knife. In a large bowl, whisk together the milk, eggs, salt, and pepper until well blended and frothy.

Lightly soak the assembled panini in the milk mixture until very moist, but not soggy. Transfer to a plate and let sit a few minutes to finish soaking.

Lightly oil the panini grill and preheat to medium. Grill the panini until the bread is golden, the egg mixture sets, and the cheese melts and barely begins to dribble out, about 10 minutes. Serve warm.

ROASTED MACKEREL PANINI

PANINI DI SGOMBRO ARROSTO serves 4

In a pinch, canned mackerel makes more than respectable panini, actually quite good. Mackerel packed in water, if drained well and seasoned well, is very good and convenient. Some folks from northern Italy like to spread a little mustard on the fish before grilling the panini—not southern Italian, but it does work. Serve with a semi-dry white wine, such as Pinot Bianco.

CONTORNO: Sliced red onions, cucumbers, a few sliced radishes, lots of chopped parsley, a clove of garlic, sea salt, freshly ground black pepper, and some red pepper flakes.

4   medium mackerel (about 1 1/2 pounds before cleaning), fresh as can be

1/2 cup extra virgin olive oil

Horseradish mustard, for the fish (optional)

Sea salt and freshly ground black pepper

3   cloves garlic, finely chopped

1   tablespoon toasted or plain sesame seeds

2   teaspoons freshly squeezed lemon juice

2   tablespoons chopped fresh Italian parsley

Clean the mackerel; remove the heads and entrails and discard. Cut along the backbone and open the fish like a book to flatten them out. Rinse the fish under cold running water and pat very dry. If there are large bones, remove them with tweezers or forceps (very fine bones are no problem to eat); or ask your fishmonger to clean the fish for you.

To cook the fish, preheat a panini grill to high. Brush the fish inside and out with 2 or 3 tablespoons of the olive oil and the mustard, if desired, and sprinkle liberally with salt and pepper. Spread, inside and out, with the 2/3 of the chopped garlic and the sesame seeds (I prefer toasted), and fold the fish closed. You

4   ciabatta rolls, halved
    lengthwise, or 1 (16-ounce)
    ciabatta loaf, cut crosswise
    into quarters, then halved
    lengthwise

can grill them opened, but that takes up too much room and the fish might cook too quickly. Place the fish on the grill and close the lid. Grill for about 4 minutes, until there are golden grill marks on the skin; longer if you think they need it. Remove from the grill and set aside on a plate. Fillet the fish, discarding the backbone and any unwanted bones. (The skin is good and should be eaten.)

In a small bowl, mix the remaining olive oil (or a bit more) with the lemon juice, chopped parsley, and remaining chopped garlic.

To assemble the panini, wipe the grill clean. Toast the rolls on the cut sides and remove. Arrange the mackerel on the bottom halves of the rolls and cover with the roll tops. Spoon the garlic mixture over the fish. Grill the panini until golden brown. Cut each panino in half for convenient eating. Eat hot.

PANINI WITH TUNA SAUCE AND SAUTÉED ONIONS *PANINI AL TONNATO E CIPOLLA IN PADELLA*

serves 4

Traditionally, *tonnato* (tuna) sauce is slathered on sliced, poached leg of veal, arranged on a large platter. But it is so good, I find people also enjoy it other ways, as a dip or in these panini. Serve with a chilled dry white wine.

CONTORNO: Sliced tomato dressed with sea salt, freshly ground black pepper, dried oregano, and a splash of red wine vinegar.

1/4 cup extra virgin olive oil

1 large onion, sliced fairly thin

1 (6-ounce) can imported Italian tuna packed in olive oil

1/3 cup mayonnaise

3 tablespoons capers, drained

4 ciabatta rolls, halved lengthwise, or 1 (16-ounce) ciabatta loaf, cut crosswise into quarters, then halved lengthwise

In a heavy skillet, heat the olive oil over medium heat. Add the onion, decrease the heat to low, and sauté, stirring and tossing often to coat the onion with oil. In about 15 minutes the onion should be golden brown and tender. Remove from the heat and set aside.

In the jar of a blender or the work bowl of a food processor fitted with the metal blade, add the tuna with its oil and the mayonnaise and blend about 1 minute, until well mixed but still slightly coarse. Add the capers and mix again for 1 more minute.

Preheat a panini press to medium-high. Spread the bottom halves of the rolls with tuna sauce, then top with onion. Cover with the roll tops. Grill until the bread is hot, golden, and marked by the grill, about 8 minutes. Cut each panino in half and serve warm.

TUNA CARPACCIO PANINI

PANINI DI CARPACCIO DI TONNO *serves 4*

Traditionally, carpaccio is thin slices of raw beef, fanned out on a plate and dressed with a tart sauce. It was named by Harry's Bar owner Guiseppe Cipriani, who was inspired by the Renaissance painter Vittore Carpaccio's colors. Nowadays, inventive chefs have taken liberties with the carpaccio "concept." These beautiful tuna panini, which I first tasted in Venice, are a delicious example of what can result. I often serve them late evening after a movie or the opera, or just to be soigné.

CONTORNO: Thickly sliced English cucumber, thickly sliced radishes, arugula, and/or watercress, dressed with extra virgin olive oil and coarsely ground black pepper.

2 tablespoons Dijon mustard

$1/4$ cup mayonnaise

4 ciabatta rolls, halved lengthwise, or 1 (16-ounce) ciabatta loaf, cut crosswise into quarters, then halved lengthwise

1 tablespoon poppy seeds

1 tablespoon sesame seeds

10 or 12 ounces finest fresh tuna (preferably sushi grade), icy cold and cut into $1/8$-inch-thick slices

Preheat a panini grill to medium. Mix the mustard and mayonnaise together—don't just smush it up. Spread the mixture on 4 of the bread slices. Sprinkle with the poppy and sesame seeds and top with the sliced tuna. Cover with the remaining bread halves. Grill until the bread is hot, golden, and marked by the grill, about 10 minutes, but not too long or you will cook the tuna.

SHRIMP AND PESTO PANINI
PANINI DI GAMBERETTI E PESTO serves 4

These panini are yet another reason why you should always have some pesto on hand. Even thawed frozen shrimp, another convenience, could work well in this recipe.

CONTORNO: Radicchio torn into small pieces and dressed with extra virgin olive oil, balsamic vinegar, sea salt, and freshly ground black pepper

4 ciabatta rolls, halved lengthwise, or 1 (16-ounce) ciabatta loaf, cut crosswise into quarters, then halved lengthwise

3 tablespoons extra virgin olive oil

16 large (21–25 count) shrimp, peeled, deveined, and halved lengthwise

Sea salt and freshly ground black pepper

¹/₃ cup Pesto (page 23)

1 firmly packed cup arugula or spinach leaves, for layering

Preheat a panini grill to high. Place the bread on the grill and toast quickly to mark with golden stripes. In a large, heavy, shallow skillet, heat the oil on medium heat. Sprinkle the shrimp with salt and pepper and add to the pan—they will curl up immediately. Gently toss the shrimp for about 2 minutes and transfer them to a plate to cool slightly. Spread a generous amount of pesto on the bottom halves of the rolls, layer on some shrimp, then divide the arugula into 4 portions and place on the shrimp. Cover with the roll tops. Cut each panino in half for convenient eating.

ANCHOVY "RED DEVIL"–STYLE PANINI

PANINI DI ACCIUGHE AL DIAVOLICCHIO serves 4

If hot is your thing, these fiery panini will fan the flames: they are salty, tasty, blazing hot, and addictive. A refreshing dry white wine, served well chilled, is a soothing counterpoint to this truly "hot" lunch.

CONTORNO: Romaine lettuce, tomato wedges, and freshly grated Parmesan, dressed with lemon juice and anchovy oil (reserved from the recipe).

2 (3.3-ounce) jars anchovy fillets, packed in extra virgin olive oil

1 teaspoon red pepper flakes

Freshly ground black pepper

4 ciabatta rolls, halved lengthwise, or 1 (16-ounce) ciabatta loaf, cut crosswise into quarters, then halved lengthwise

¼ cup coarsely chopped fresh Italian parsley

Gently remove the anchovies from the jar and lay them separately on a large plate with about half their oil. (Reserve the remaining oil for the *contorno*.) Sprinkle the red pepper flakes evenly over the anchovies; season with a nice amount of black pepper. Let the anchovies marinate for at least 2 hours at room temperature. (You can marinate them 1 or 2 days ahead, stored in the refrigerator, well covered. They must be brought to room temperature to be enjoyed.)

Preheat a panini grill to high. Place the bread on the grill and toast quickly on both sides to mark lightly with golden stripes. Arrange 6 (or more) fillets with the pepper flakes and pepper on 4 of the bread slices, and sprinkle with chopped parsley. Cover with the remaining bread and gently press down. Serve each panino cut in half or thirds.

FRESH TUNA "HAMBURGER"
AMBURGESE DI TONNO FRESCO serves 4

Sicilians eat tuna that is mostly conserved, either from home supplies or bought in tins. When they eat tuna fresh (and they do), they like it grilled or pan-fried and well cooked. But the Sicilians to whom I have fed these panini *amburgese* are quite tickled. They declare them "so American," so "novel," "very modern," and utterly delicious! If you wish, you could serve the watercress as a side instead of as part of the panini.

CONTORNO: Watercress dressed with lemon vinaigrette (see page 22).

1   pound fresh tuna

2   cloves garlic, finely chopped

¹/₄ teaspoon red pepper flakes

1   tablespoon capers, drained

¹/₂ teaspoon sea salt

¹/₄ teaspoon freshly ground black pepper

Grated zest of 1 orange

3   tablespoons fresh or dry bread crumbs

¹/₂ cup extra virgin olive oil

4   ciabatta rolls, halved lengthwise, or 1 (16-ounce) ciabatta loaf, cut crosswise into quarters, then halved lengthwise

To make the tuna patties, using a sharp, heavy knife, chop the tuna by hand to the texture of hamburger meat. Do not use a food processor, or you will smash it. In a bowl, combine the tuna, garlic, red pepper flakes, capers, ¹/₄ teaspoon of the salt, black pepper, orange zest, bread crumbs, and 2 tablespoons of the olive oil. Gently toss the ingredients with your hands or a fork to keep them light and fluffy. Carefully form the mixture into 4 patties, each about 1 inch thick; set aside. In a wide, heavy skillet, heat 2 tablespoons, or a bit more, of the olive oil on medium heat. Pan-fry the tuna patties until the exterior is no longer red, about 2 minutes on each side, less time if you like your tuna more rare.

continued

To assemble the panini, preheat a panini grill to high. Toast the bread quickly on both sides to mark lightly with golden stripes. Place a tuna patty on the bottom half of each roll. Cover with the roll tops and gently press closed. Cut each panino in half for convenient eating. The panini are best when freshly made, but can sit for up to 1 hour and be eaten at room temperature.

PAN-ROASTED HALIBUT (SEA-SPARROW) AND CARAMELIZED TOMATO PANINI

PANINI DI PÀSSERA DI MARE (IPPOGLOSSO) ARROSTO

serves 4

I love fresh halibut, especially if it is wild. The flavor is fresher and sweeter and the texture is much more enjoyable than the frozen kind.

Roasting the tomatoes caramelizes their natural sugars, making them taste sweeter. Their lush flavor complements the taste and texture of the halibut. Any extra roasted tomatoes can be combined with a couple of teaspoons of balsamic vinegar, lightly mashed with a fork, and used as a kind of relish.

CONTORNO: Mixed Green Salad (page 21).

¹/₃ cup extra virgin olive oil

2 large tomatoes, cored and cut crosswise into ¹/₂-inch-thick slices

Preheat the oven to 500°F. To caramelize the tomatoes, brush a heavy roasting pan with a generous amount of the olive oil. Season the tomato slices on

Salt and freshly ground black
   pepper

2 tablespoons fresh
   rosemary, finely chopped

1 large clove garlic, finely
   chopped

4 ciabatta rolls, halved
   lengthwise, or 1 (16-ounce)
   ciabatta loaf, cut crosswise
   into quarters, then halved
   lengthwise

1 pound freshest halibut,
   skin on, cut into 4 equal
   pieces

About 14 large basil leaves,
   torn by hand

both sides with salt and pepper; arrange them about
$^1/_2$ inch apart in the roasting pan and scatter on the
rosemary and garlic. Roast the tomatoes until they
are very dark with little burnt spots all over, about 15
minutes. Remove from the oven and cool. You can
also cook them on a panini grill preheated to its highest setting. Grill the tomatoes until caramelized as
described, about 12 minutes.

To prepare the panini, clean the grill and lightly toast
the bread on both sides until just golden. Put about
3 tablespoons of the olive oil in a heavy skillet over
high heat. Generously season the halibut with salt
and pepper. Set it in the hot skillet, skin side down,
and fry for about 3 minutes, or until the skin is dark
and crunchy. Turn the fish over and cook 1 minute
more. Halibut is meaty and dense, and it can be dry,
so it is a good idea to slightly undercook it; medium-
rare is best. Place a piece of fish on the bottom half of
each roll, then some caramelized tomatoes and some
of the basil. Cover with the roll tops, gently pressing
closed. Cut each panino in half with a sharp knife if
you wish, and serve.

EGGS "BENEDICT" PANINI
PANINI UOVA BENEDETTO serves 4

My friends kid me about ciabatta being the new "Italian muffin." These are amazing panini and everyone enjoys them, raving about how good they are. The shape and color of the pancetta (see page 6), a porky pinwheel, are beautiful, and you should try to keep its lovely rolled-up shape when you cook and serve it. Prosecco, a sparkling wine from the Veneto, is a festive accompaniment.

If you do not use spanking fresh eggs, they will spread out when they hit the simmering water. They will be edible but not as pretty and firm and tender as they might be.

CONTORNO: Gaeta olives and peeled orange segments.

Extra virgin olive oil

8 very thin slices pancetta, cut like bacon but kept in round shape

4 cups water

Salt and freshly ground black pepper

3 tablespoons distilled white vinegar or freshly squeezed lemon juice

8 large eggs, as fresh as possible

In a large, heavy, shallow skillet, heat 2 teaspoons of the oil over medium heat. Shape the pancetta into a circle as it was originally cured.

Fry the slices, a few at a time, in the hot pan until they are golden brown, firm, and crunchy, about 6 minutes. Drain on paper towels. Set aside. (These can be made up to a day ahead and stored in the refrigerator, well covered.)

To poach the eggs, wipe out the pan used to fry the pancetta of any excess fat, or use another frying pan rubbed with a tablespoon or so of olive oil on a paper towel.

- 2 cups heavy cream
- 1 tablespoon fresh rosemary leaves, finely chopped (about 1 medium branch)
- 4 ciabatta rolls, halved lengthwise, or 1 (16-ounce) ciabatta loaf, cut crosswise into quarters, then halved lengthwise
- About 10 fresh basil leaves, cut in julienne, for garnish

Add the 4 cups of water, a teaspoonful of salt, and the vinegar and stir to mix. Bring to a heavy simmer over medium heat. Working with 1 egg at a time, break the egg into a flat, rimmed dish or a small bowl, then gently slip the intact egg into the simmering water. (You can do up to 4 eggs at a time—more is difficult.) When the whites begin to set, about 30 seconds, gently push them against the yolks to make a nice shape. Simmer about 2 minutes, or until the whites are quite firm. Gently remove the eggs from the water with a slotted spoon and lay them on a flat plate. This keeps them from cooking further. Continue until all the eggs are cooked.

Reserve the cooking water for finishing the eggs. (You can cook the eggs up to 2 days ahead; store them on paper towels in a covered dish and refrigerate until needed.) To make the sauce, in a small, heavy saucepan, simmer the cream over medium heat until it is reduced by one-third, about 8 minutes, depending on your pan and your heat source. Add the rosemary, season with salt and pepper, and keep the sauce warm.

continued

Have individual heated plates ready. When ready to serve, preheat a panini grill to high. Toast the bread quickly to mark with golden stripes here and there. Do not let it dry out; it should be toasted on the outside but tender in the middle. Place the bottom halves of the rolls on warm plates. Bring the water back to a simmer and add the reserved eggs. Cook them another 1 to 2 minutes (more if you do not like runny yolks, but not more than 3 minutes). With a slotted spoon, momentarily drain eggs on paper towels to rid them of excess water. Transfer 1 egg to each piece of bread and generously spoon on some of the rosemary cream. Garnish each piece of bread with a pancetta spiral. Place the roll tops alongside. Sprinkle on some of the julienned basil and serve immediately.

PANINI WITH MORTADELLA, SALAMI, AND CELERY PANINI DI MORTADELLA, SALAME, E SEDANO

serves 4

In Bologna, where I have eaten these panini often, the celery is white and very tender, whereas here, it is a darker green and not nearly as tender. Bologna is also noted for its sublime mortadella. If you can find it, I recommend using Italian mortadella with pistachio nuts, which is now available in many American markets. Use the smallest, most tender celery you can find, the tender yellow heart being the best part.

CONTORNO: Sliced tomatoes seasoned with sea salt, freshly ground black pepper, and extra virgin olive oil.

Unsalted butter, at cold room temperature, for spreading

4 ciabatta rolls, halved lengthwise, or ¾ ciabatta loaf, cut crosswise into 4 4-inch slices, then halved lengthwise

3 long, inner, yellow stalks celery, sliced into very long diagonal pieces, ⅛ to ¼ inch thick

4 ounces mortadella, thinly sliced

4 ounces salami, thinly sliced

Spread a thin layer of butter on both cut sides of the rolls (this will help hold the sliced celery in place). Scatter the celery pieces all over the butter on the bottom halves, then add a layer each of mortadella and salami. Cover with the roll tops, gently pat closed, and cut each panino in half for convenient eating.

PROSCIUTTO AND MELON PANINI
PANINI DI PROSCIUTTO E MELONE serves 4

Good prosciutto is readily available around the country now. When I have some, along with a good melon, I often make these panini for a refreshing small meal. It is practically no work, it looks beautiful, and the flavor combination is sensational. Even for a small meal, the luscious taste of the prosciutto with the melon is very satisfying.

CONTORNO: Dried figs or dates.

4   ciabatta rolls, halved lengthwise, or 1 (16-ounce) ciabatta loaf, cut crosswise into quarters, then halved lengthwise

1   cantaloupe (about 3 pounds), dead-ripe and fragrant

12 thin slices prosciutto di Parma or San Daniele

Freshly ground black pepper

About 10 large fresh mint leaves, cut in julienne

Preheat a panini grill to high. Toast the bread quickly until marked with golden stripes. Peel and seed the melon, and cut the flesh into $1/2$-inch-thick slices. Layer 3 slices of prosciutto on the bottom half of each roll, then several slices of melon, some pepper, and the chopped mint. Cover with the roll tops. Toast in the panini grill on high for about 10 minutes, just to heat the outside of the bread. Cut each panino in half for convenient eating.

PORTOBELLO MUSHROOM AND FRESH THYME
PANINI PANINI DI FUNGHI PORTOBELLO E TIMO

serves 4

These are among my very favorite panini, great for vegetarians. Portobello mushrooms have a deep woodsy, earthy taste that makes them very popular. The flavors go well with pesto and sliced tomatoes. You could serve the arugula separately, if you wish, lightly dressed in a vinaigrette (see page 22).

CONTORNO: Celery sticks, parsley stalks, and Belgian endive leaves.

4   large young, firm portobello mushrooms (about 8 ounces)

Extra virgin olive oil

Salt and freshly ground black pepper

1/3 small bunch fresh thyme

4   ciabatta rolls, halved lengthwise, or 1 (16-ounce) ciabatta loaf, cut crosswise into quarters, then halved lengthwise

1/4 cup Pesto (page 23; optional)

2   cups arugula leaves, for layering

1   small red onion, thinly sliced

1/2 teaspoon red pepper flakes

Remove the large stems from the mushrooms and chop the stems very finely. Set aside. Slather the caps with plenty of olive oil, and season with salt and pepper. Scatter the thyme leaves all over the mushroom caps, both top and bottom (gill) sides. Preheat a panini grill or broiler to high. Cook the mushrooms for about 10 minutes, or until they are slightly soft, turning once. Set aside.

If you used your panini grill, let it cool and clean it, wiping it with paper towels. Set it on high, or use the broiler or a toaster. Toast the bread on both sides to mark with golden stripes. To assemble the panini, spread some pesto on the bottom halves of the rolls

continued

and top each with a roasted mushroom cap. Scatter on the chopped raw mushroom stems, then some arugula leaves, sliced red onion, and plenty of red pepper flakes. Cover with the roll tops. Gently heat the panini in the panini grill or in a hot oven, about 10 minutes. Cut in half for convenient eating. Serve hot.

HONEY AND PECORINO FRESCO CHEESE
PANINI *PANINI DI MIELE E PECORINO FRESCO* serves 4

Italians like to drizzle honey on cheeses. In Sardinia, among the heavenly "desserts" enjoyed as a snack in the middle of the morning or afternoon are *pardulas* (or *sebadas*), cheese-filled pastries coated with the most exotic honey imaginable. Here, we have a version made with bread. It is fantastic with a dry red or white wine, or a dry, nutty vin santo. These make a delicious nibble before a concert or movie and add Mediterranean flair to a picnic.

CONTORNO: Wedges of sweet-tart apple (such as Fuji or Braeburn), unpeeled if the skin is nice and bright.

4 ciabatta rolls, halved lengthwise, or 1 (16-ounce) ciabatta loaf, cut crosswise into quarters, then halved lengthwise

1/4 cup bitter honey, such as chestnut blossom (fior' di castagno)

4 ounces pecorino or Asiago fresco, thinly sliced, or soft goat cheese

About 1 ounce toasted walnuts or hazelnuts, coarsely chopped (optional)

Coarsely ground black pepper (optional)

Preheat a panini grill to high. Toast the bread to make nice golden stripes here and there. Spread honey on the bottom halves of the rolls and top with a few slices of cheese. (If you use goat cheese, spread it on the cut sides of the roll tops.) Scatter on the nuts, sprinkle with plenty of black pepper, and cover with the remaining bread. Cut each panino in half for convenient eating.

OPEN-FACED WAFFLE PANINI PANINI "AWFUL"

serves 4

My mother could never say "waffle," so her version, made with bread and with Pa's old and wonderful iron, was invariably "awful." These are anything but.

If you don't have a waffle iron, use your panini grill to toast the bread and just scatter the ingredients on. Vary some of the fillings as you like. I recommend capers, finely chopped red onion, chopped green or black olives, or chopped parsley. Try to find anchovies packed with black truffle, which have an earthy, almost musty flavor. Serve with a big, rich red wine.

CONTORNO: Thinly sliced raw bulb fennel, pickled cherry peppers, whole radishes, or sliced turnips.

4   1-inch-thick slices ciabatta bread

Extra virgin olive oil

1   (3.3-ounce) jar anchovy fillets packed in extra virgin olive oil, drained and chopped into 1/4-inch pieces, oil reserved

2   ounces Pecorino Sardo or Romano cheese, diced

1/2 teaspoon fennel seeds, crushed

1   medium tomato, cored and finely diced

Freshly ground black pepper

If the bread is flat, such as ciabatta often is, and the slices seem inadequate, use more of them, perhaps twice as many. You should have enough ingredients, but you can increase them easily.

Preheat a waffle maker to high. Set the bread on the lower grid and close the lid firmly (you may have to hold down the lid with your hand for a few minutes to impress the grid holes into the bread). Cook until the bread turns golden brown, 8 to 10 minutes. When done, remove the bread and immediately drizzle on

continued

plenty of the oil, as evenly as you can, including some of the reserved anchovy oil (use any remaining oil to dress salads or brush on cold leftover fish). Fill most of the holes with some anchovy, diced pecorino, crushed fennel seeds, and diced tomato. Shower the whole surface of the "awfuls" with black pepper. Eat hot.

SOFT GOAT CHEESE AND RADICCHIO PANINI

PANINI DI CAPRINO E RADICCHIO serves 4

The goat cheese–radicchio filling is simple to make and can be done a day ahead. Assemble the panini when you are ready to serve. You can substitute poppy seeds for sesame seeds, if you prefer, as they do in the north of Italy.

CONTORNO: Sliced pear and toasted hazelnuts.

4   ciabatta rolls, halved lengthwise, or 1 (16-ounce) ciabatta loaf, cut crosswise into quarters, then halved lengthwise

1   medium (about 8 ounces) head of radicchio, preferably Trevisano, trimmed and sliced as thinly as possible

2   tablespoons extra virgin olive oil

Coarsely ground black pepper

1   large clove garlic, finely chopped

2   teaspoons toasted sesame seeds

4   ounces soft goat cheese

Preheat a panini grill to high. Toast the bread to make golden stripes here and there. Place the radicchio in a bowl and add the olive oil, pepper, garlic, and sesame seeds; mix well. Gently fold the goat cheese into the radicchio mixture. Using a fork, spread the radicchio mixture on the bottom halves of the rolls. Cover with the roll tops and press gently to close. Slice each panino in half and eat immediately.

SCRAMBLED EGG AND TOMATO PANINI
PANINI DI UOVA STRAPAZZATI serves 4

On many a school day, these panini were my lunch. They are versatile, and very tasty. At brunch or on a picnic, for their speed and ease of making, these panini hold a special place for me as my childhood comfort food.

CONTORNO: Chilled yellow butter lettuce leaves, served with a mixture of chopped green onion, chopped raw garlic, a few capers, and sea salt and freshly ground black pepper spooned on top.

4 ciabatta rolls, halved lengthwise, or 1 (16-ounce) ciabatta loaf, cut crosswise into quarters, then halved lengthwise

¼ cup extra virgin olive oil

6 large eggs, as fresh as possible

Sea salt and freshly ground black pepper

2 medium tomatoes, cored, peeled, and cut into ¼-inch dice

Preheat a panini grill to high. Toast the bread to make nice golden stripes here and there.

In a large, heavy skillet, heat plenty of olive oil over medium heat. Break the eggs into a large, flat soup bowl and add some salt and pepper. With a fork, beat *very lightly and very quickly!*—3 or 4 strokes only; *don't overmix them*, or they will look like a monotonous yellow cushion. Put the tomatoes in the warmed oil, toss in the beaten eggs, and let the eggs set for about 20 seconds. Gently stir and toss for another 1 to 2 minutes. The eggs should be soft and fluffy, and if made right, the egg-tomato mixture will resemble a stained-glass window. If you overcook the eggs, they will taste chalky instead of sublime. If you want to

continued

cut the panini in half for ease of eating, do so before adding the eggs, or you will squash them out of the panini. Immediately divide the eggs evenly among the roll bottoms; cover with the roll tops. Serve hot, but these are delicious at room temperature, too.

FOUR-CHEESE PANINI

PANINI AI QUATTRO FORMAGGI serves 4

You can make these panini with three of the cheeses, but I would keep the Gorgonzola as one of them—it has a real flavor appeal. These grilled panini travel well and are ideal for a picnic or a casual garden meal.

CONTORNO: Celery sticks, large green olives, and green onions.

4 ounces shredded or sliced fresh mozzarella cheese

4 ounces shredded or sliced fontina cheese

4 ounces shredded or sliced provolone cheese

2 ounces crumbled Gorgonzola cheese

4 ciabatta rolls, halved lengthwise, or 8 ³/₄-inch-thick slices whole-wheat country bread

About 24 large arugula leaves

If you are using shredded mozzarella, fontina, and provolone, combine them in a small bowl along with the Gorgonzola and spread on the bottom halves of the rolls. (If you use sliced cheese, simply layer them and scatter on the Gorgonzola.) Top the cheese with several arugula leaves. Cover with the roll tops. Preheat a panini grill to moderately high. Toast the panini until the bread has golden stripes and is quite warm so that the cheese melts a little, about 10 minutes. Do not let it get too hot or the cheese will run out. Cut each panino in half for convenient eating.

PIEDMONT-STYLE FONTINA CHEESE, LETTUCE, AND CELERY PANINI PANINI ALLA PIEMONTESE

serves 4

If you have some good Piemonte cheese like fontina, you can make these panini in a flash. They are perfect for afternoon tea. I like them best with a dry white wine.

CONTORNO: Olive-oil-packed anchovies sprinkled with red pepper flakes, finely chopped Italian parsley, and a few slices of garlic.

Unsalted butter, at cold room temperature, for spreading

4   ciabatta rolls, halved lengthwise, or 1 (16-ounce) ciabatta loaf, cut crosswise into quarters, then halved lengthwise

4   long, inner, yellow stalks celery, sliced into very long diagonal pieces, $1/8$ to $1/4$ inch thick

4   ounces sliced or shredded Fontina Valdostana cheese

1   small head of butter lettuce, separated into leaves

Salt and freshly ground black pepper

1   teaspoon white truffle oil

1   tablespoon extra virgin olive oil

Spread a thin layer of butter on the bottom halves of the rolls. Scatter the celery pieces over the butter and gently press to hold them in place. Add a layer of cheese and 2 or 3 lettuce leaves. Season with salt and a generous amount of pepper. Mix together the truffle and olive oils. Drizzle the oils over the cut sides of the roll tops. Set the tops on the sandwiches and gently press closed. Cut each panino in half for convenient eating.

CAVIAR PANINI PANINI AL CAVIALE serves 4

The Romans were masters at curing caviar and feasted on it regularly. Nowadays, the cost of caviar is an emperor's ransom (as opposed to a mere king's ransom), yet Italians still love it and have many delicious ways of serving it. I like to serve these panini open-faced, 2 slices per person. The presentation is very dramatic and makes *la bella figura*. These panini call for prosecco or a dry white wine.

CONTORNO: Radicchio and cabbage tossed in a lemon juice vinaigrette (see page 22).

3/4 ciabatta loaf, cut crosswise into 4 3-inch slices, then halved lengthwise

4 ounces soft mild goat cheese

1/2 small red onion, very finely chopped

2 tablespoons finely chopped fresh Italian parsley

Freshly ground black pepper

Grated zest of 1 lemon

Sea salt

4 ounces salmon roe, tobiko roe, or lumpfish caviar, or 2 ounces sevruga caviar

Preheat a panini grill to high. In a bowl, fold together the goat cheese, onion, parsley, plenty of black pepper, and lemon zest (do not overmix). Taste the mix. It should not need any salt, since the caviar is salty, but if it does, add to taste. Lightly toast the bread until it is marked with golden stripes here and there. While the bread is still warm, spread a layer of cheese mixture on 4 pieces of the bread. Spoon on some caviar and cover with the remaining slices. Gently press to close. Alternatively, to serve the panini open-faced, spread a layer of cheese mixture on all 8 slices of bread and spoon some caviar on top. Cut each panino in half for convenient eating.

BROCCOLI RABE, BLACK OLIVE, AND GARLIC
PANINI PANINI DI RAPINI, OLIVE NERI, ED AGLIO

serves 4

Everything about these panini is delicious: the rapini are fantastically green and inviting, punctuated with black olives, garlic, and sausage. The flavors, intense on their own, become as one when mixed. I prefer these panini plain rather than toasted, but it's up to you. If made without sausage, they are very tasty treats for vegetarians. Serve with a heavy red wine.

CONTORNO: Peeled orange segments topped with julienne-cut mint and sliced green onions.

8   ounces (2 links) uncooked Italian fennel or plain sausage (optional)

1   bunch broccoli rabe (about 12 ounces), trimmed and cut into 3-inch pieces

Extra virgin olive oil

3   cloves garlic, thinly sliced

4   ounces pitted black olives (such as Gaeta or oil-cured)

Pinch of red pepper flakes

4   ciabatta rolls, halved lengthwise, or 1 (16-ounce) ciabatta loaf, cut crosswise into quarters, then halved lengthwise

To roast the sausage, preheat the oven to 375°F. Put the links in an ovenproof pan and roast until dark gold, about 25 minutes. Prick with a fork; if the juice runs clear they should be done. Let cool for about 5 minutes and slice or coarsely chop. Set aside and keep warm.

To cook the greens, in a heavy saucepan bring lightly salted water to a boil over medium-high heat. Add the broccoli rabe and cook for 3 to 5 minutes, until al dente. Drain well and set aside.

continued

In a heavy skillet, heat the olive oil over medium heat. Sauté the garlic until lightly golden, about 2 minutes; toss in the broccoli rabe and the olives, and stir well. Add a big pinch of red pepper flakes and stir again. Mix in the sausage and stir until heated.

Preheat a panini grill to high. Lightly toast the bread to mark with golden stripes here and there. Divide the broccoli mixture among the bottom halves of the rolls. Cover with the roll tops and press gently to close or place the tops on the side. Cut each panino in half for convenient eating and serve.

SLICED DRESSED RAW MUSHROOMS PANINI

PANINI DI FUNGHI ALLA CRUDAIOLO serves 4

This is one of my favorite dishes. Thinly sliced mushrooms prepared like *funghi al funghetto* (see page 88), but raw, are not only good in panini, but also make a terrific side dish to roasted fish or chicken or stuffed into ripe tomato halves. You can make the mushroom mixture a few hours ahead, but do not refrigerate.

CONTORNO: Thinly sliced salami and cubed Asiago or Montasio cheese.

4   ounces medium crimini
    mushrooms or assorted
    wild mushrooms (such as
    fresh porcini, chanterelle,
    hedgehog, or tree oyster),
    cut into 1/8-inch-thick slices

2   large cloves garlic, sliced
    paper-thin

1/4 cup extra virgin olive oil

1/4 bunch Italian parsley,
    chopped medium-fine

Zest and juice of 1 lemon

Salt and freshly ground black
    pepper

Pinch of red pepper flakes
    (optional)

4   ciabatta rolls, halved
    lengthwise, or 1 (16-ounce)
    ciabatta loaf, cut crosswise
    into quarters, then halved
    lengthwise

In a bowl, combine the mushrooms, garlic, olive oil, parsley, lemon zest and juice, salt, pepper, and a generous pinch of red pepper flakes. There should be plenty of juice. It must be very moist, but not like a soup.

Preheat a panini grill to high. Toast the bread on both sides until marked with golden stripes. Divide the mushroom mixture among 4 of the bread slices. Top with the remaining bread and very gently press closed. Cut each panino in half for convenient eating.

ORANGE AND ONION SALAD PANINI

PANINI DI ARANCE E CIPOLLE *serves 4*

Very refreshing on their own, these panini also make a delicious finger-food side dish to a main course. At home or on a picnic, I love them as part of a light lunch with broiled chicken. They are also a great accompaniment to roast pork.

Blood oranges, plentiful during the cold months, are the most delicious. Out of season, other oranges will work, but use more onion, mint, and parsley to compensate for their extra sweetness. A crisp white wine is called for here.

CONTORNO: Green Sicilian olives and additional orange slices.

4 ciabatta rolls, halved lengthwise, or 1 (16-ounce) ciabatta loaf, cut crosswise into quarters, then halved lengthwise

3 medium blood or navel oranges, peeled, pith removed, and cut crosswise into ¼-inch-thick slices

1 small red onion, very thinly sliced

16 fresh mint leaves

¼ cup chopped fresh Italian parsley

Salt and freshly ground black pepper

Preheat a panini grill to high. Lightly toast the bread on the uncut sides only to mark with golden stripes. Layer the bottom halves of the rolls, toasted sides down, with orange and onion slices, scatter on plenty of mint and parsley, and season generously with salt and pepper. Cover with the roll tops, toasted sides up, and gently press together. Cut each panino in half for convenient eating.

GRILLED VEGETABLE PANINI
PANINI DI VERDURE GRIGLIATE serves 4

Every Italian who comes to visit me on a casual basis lives on these—they even beg for more. Grill more vegetables than you need; you will eat them in all kinds of ways. Five or six finely chopped anchovy fillets mixed into the vinaigrette make a delicious and appreciated addition—and a typical Italian taste treat. A stout red wine is the best thing to go with these outstanding panini.

CONTORNO: Arugula, dressed with a little orange juice, extra virgin olive oil, sea salt and freshly ground black pepper, and green Sicilian-style olives.

2   small zucchini (about 6 ounces), tops and bottoms trimmed, cut into 1/4-inch-thick slices

1   medium eggplant (about 12 ounces), cut into 8 1/4-inch-thick slices

1   medium red onion, cut into 1/4-inch-thick slices

1   large red or yellow bell pepper, cored, seeded, and cut into 1-inch-wide strips

1/2 large bulb fennel, trimmed and thinly sliced (less than 1/4 inch thick)

1/2 cup extra virgin olive oil

Salt and freshly ground black pepper

Have a large, flat platter ready. To grill the vegetables, heat a panini grill, stovetop grill, or outdoor grill until quite hot. Place the zucchini, eggplant, onion, bell pepper, and fennel in a large bowl. Add about 3 tablespoons of the olive oil and some salt and pepper; toss well to coat. Grill each vegetable separately, until deep grill marks appear and they soften a bit (do not overcook them), turning them once, about 6 minutes total for each. As you finish each vegetable, put them on the platter, slightly overlapping. Continue until you have grilled them all.

continued

- ¹/₄ cup red wine vinegar
- 1 teaspoon dried oregano
- 4 ciabatta rolls, halved lengthwise, or 1 (16-ounce) ciabatta loaf, cut crosswise into quarters, then halved lengthwise
- 2 large cloves garlic, peeled

To make the vinaigrette, mix the vinegar with about ¹/₃ cup (or more) of the olive oil, the oregano, and some salt and pepper. Splash this all over the grilled vegetables, and let rest for at least a few minutes (a few hours is even better).

To assemble the panini, grill the bread on both sides to mark with golden stripes, and rub 1 side with the peeled garlic cloves. Drizzle generous amounts of the olive oil on the side you rubbed with garlic. Divide the vegetables among the bottom halves of the rolls and cover with the roll tops. Cut each panino in half for convenient eating.

HERBED FRITTATA PANINI
PANINI DI FRITTATA D'ERBE serves 4

You can vary the herbs—basil and oregano, for example, or rosemary and thyme. But mint is my favorite. One caution: Do not be heavy-handed with the herbs. You want a hint of taste, not an explosion. As with any frittata, the panini are good hot or at room temperature, and make tasty picnic food.

CONTORNO: Tomato, cucumber, and dried oregano salad dressed with Basic Vinaigrette (page 22).

4 large eggs

About 14 large fresh mint leaves, finely chopped

1/4 bunch Italian parsley, chopped medium-fine

1/4 cup freshly grated dry pecorino cheese

2 tablespoons dry bread crumbs

3 tablespoons extra virgin olive oil

Salt and freshly ground black pepper

4 ciabatta rolls, halved lengthwise

To make the frittata, break the eggs into a large, shallow bowl and gently whisk, but not too much. Add the mint, parsley, cheese, and bread crumbs, and mix again. In a large, shallow skillet, heat the oil over medium heat until hot but not smoking, about 3 minutes. Add the egg mixture and let it set for about 20 seconds; lower the heat slightly to keep the egg mixture from browning too fast or burning. Gently scrape the sides of the eggs toward the center of the pan; keep doing this until the top looks somewhat set. Cover the skillet with a large plate, holding the plate securely with your hand. Turn the frying pan and plate over so that the frittata slips out onto the plate. Carefully and gently slide the frittata back into the pan to cook on the bottom. The total cooking time should be about 6 minutes. You can also finish the frittata in a preheated 375°F oven; bake 15 minutes, or until the top is uniformly deep gold and slightly firm to the touch. Or, you could carefully broil the top until deep gold and just set.

Preheat a panini grill to high. Toast the bread quickly to mark with golden stripes. Cut the frittata any way you like, set the pieces on the roll bottoms, and cover with the roll tops. Cut each panino in half for convenient eating. Serve hot or at room temperature.

"MUSHROOMS COOKED LIKE MUSHROOMS," GARLIC, AND PARSLEY PANINI

PANINI DI FUNGHI AL FUNGHETTO serves 4

The whimsy of Italian names for food is evident here. This method works beautifully with a variety of vegetables, not just mushrooms. Simply substitute eggplant, zucchini, or bulb fennel for the mushrooms and proceed. *Ecco!* You have *funghetto*.

CONTORNO: Thinly sliced soppressata and pecorino fresco cheese.

¼ cup extra virgin olive oil

3 large cloves garlic, sliced paper-thin

8 ounces medium crimini mushrooms or assorted wild mushrooms (such as fresh porcini, chanterelle, hedgehog, or tree oyster), cut into ⅛-inch-thick slices

¼ bunch Italian parsley, chopped medium-fine

Salt and freshly ground black pepper

Pinch of red pepper flakes (optional)

4 ciabatta rolls, halved lengthwise, or 1 (16-ounce) ciabatta loaf, cut crosswise into quarters, then halved lengthwise

In a large, heavy skillet, heat the olive oil over medium heat. Toss in the garlic and sauté until it is just golden and fragrant, about 1 minute. Add the sliced mushrooms and quickly stir. Lower the heat a bit and cook the mushrooms until they are soft and fragrant, about 6 minutes. Stir in the parsley, salt, black pepper, and a generous pinch of red pepper flakes if you like, and cook a minute longer.

Preheat a panini grill to high. Toast the bread on both sides until marked with golden stripes. Divide the mushroom mixture among the bottoms of the rolls. Cover with the roll tops and very gently press closed. Cut each panino in half for convenient eating. Eat hot or at room temperature.

CHICKPEA CRÊPE AND POTATO CROQUETTE (LITTLE PRICKS) PANINI

PANINI DI PANELLE E CAZZILLI serves 4

These famous Sicilian panini, with their naughty name, are sinfully good. In Palermo, I have been known to eat them at least once a day. *Panelle* are delicious fritters that resemble little flat breads made from chickpea flour. *Cazzilli* are addictive little potato croquettes.

The *panelle* and *cazzilli* are best served immediately but can be made a day ahead and reheated in a 375°F oven for about 10 minutes. The *panelle* recipe makes about 30.

CONTORNO: Peeled orange chunks, green Sicilian olives, chopped green onions, and sliced radishes or turnips, dusted with sea salt and freshly ground black pepper, and dressed with lemon juice and extra virgin olive oil.

PANELLE

- 3 cups chickpea flour
- 4 cups water
- Sea salt and freshly ground black pepper
- 3 tablespoons finely minced fresh parsley or oregano
- 2 cups extra virgin olive oil or vegetable oil, for frying
- 1 lemon, cut into wedges, for squeezing

To make the panelle: Lightly oil a 9 by 12-inch jelly-roll pan and set aside. Place a heavy-bottomed saucepan over medium heat. Add the chickpea flour, then slowly add the water, whisking in one direction only to assure there will be no lumps. Add salt and pepper to taste and cook for about 12 minutes, stirring constantly, until the batter is thick and starts to pull away from the sides of the pan. Add the parsley and cook for 2 or 3 minutes.

continued

CAZZILLI

2 cups leftover cooked mashed potatoes

3 tablespoons freshly grated pecorino cheese

2 tablespoons chopped fresh Italian parsley

1 large clove garlic, peeled and finely chopped

Sea salt and freshly ground black pepper

2 egg whites

1 cup dry bread crumbs, or more as needed

2 cups extra virgin olive oil or vegetable oil, for frying

4 ciabatta rolls, halved lengthwise, or 1 (16-ounce) ciabatta loaf, cut crosswise into quarters, then halved lengthwise

Quickly pour the contents onto the lightly oiled jelly-roll pan and spread evenly to less than $^1/_4$ inch thick using a metal spatula dipped frequently in warm water. Work fast to keep the batter from stiffening and deforming. Let cool for about 1 hour at room temperature, until set. Cut into pieces about 2 by 3 inches in size.

Heat the oil in a deep frying pan to 375°F. The oil should be deep enough to completely cover the panelle, so choose your pan accordingly and use more oil if needed. Fry the panelle a few at a time for about 2 minutes on each side, until light gold. Drain on paper towels. Keep the already fried ones warm in a hot oven with the door ajar. While the panelle are still piping hot, squeeze on a bit of lemon juice, and sprinkle liberally with salt. You may reserve the oil to fry the cazzilli. (The oil, if not overheated, can be used 3 or 4 times as long as it is clean and clear.) Keep the panelle warm until ready to serve.

To make the cazzilli: In a bowl, combine the potatoes, cheese, parsley, garlic, and salt and pepper, and mix well. Form into rods about 1 inch thick and 3 inches long, or about the size of your middle finger. Carefully roll the cazzilli in the egg white, and then coat with bread crumbs.

In the same skillet used to fry the panelle (if you wish), and using the same oil if it is clean, add enough oil to fill the pan to a depth of $^1/_2$ inch; set over medium heat. When the oil is hot, slip in a few cazzilli at a time, and fry until they are light golden, turning them once, about 3 minutes.

To assemble the panini, preheat a panini grill to high. Lightly toast the bread on both sides until just golden. Put 2 or more cazzilli on each of the bottom halves of the rolls, then 3 or 4 pieces of panelle. If you have not done so already, squeeze on some lemon juice, and sprinkle with salt to taste. Cover with the roll tops, cut each in half, and eat immediately.

SWEET
PANINI

panini dolci

CHOCOLATE PANINI PANINI DI CIOCCOLATO

serves 4

In Italy, these goodies are saved for mid-morning or mid-afternoon snacks to enjoy with coffee or grappa, or even hot chocolate, but they are also perfect for tea. If you feel the need for a "sauce," a dollop of plain mascarpone cheese is my choice. Whip it first to soften it, and allow about 2 tablespoonfuls per serving.

Chocolate with 60 to 72 percent cacao is best. Avoid chocolate with heavy cocoa butter content, which is better suited for tempering to make fancy chocolate molds or to give special gloss to cakes or candies.

CONTORNO: Fresh, very cold sliced ripe cantaloupe or strawberries.

8 $1/2$-inch-thick slices
   ciabatta bread

6 ounces bittersweet
   chocolate, chopped
   medium-fine

Zest of 1 orange

$1/4$ cup toasted hazelnuts
   or almonds, chopped
   (optional)

Unsalted butter, at room
   temperature, for spreading

Mascarpone cheese, whipped,
   for topping (optional)

Preheat a panini grill to medium-high. Toast the bread on one side to mark with golden stripes. Sprinkle the toasted sides of 4 of the bread slices with chocolate, then scatter on the orange zest and nuts if you wish. Cover with the remaining bread slices, toasted side down. Lightly butter the untoasted surfaces of the bread. Grill the panini until the bread is lightly toasted and the chocolate melts, but does not run out. Cut each panino in half for easier eating either diagonally or in rectangles, and serve warm. You can top them with a little whipped mascarpone if you like.

GOAT CHEESE AND RASPBERRY OPEN-FACED
PANINI PANINI APERTI DI FORMAGGIO DI CAPRA E LAMPONE serves 4

These beautiful and tasty panini are an always-welcome snack, and served with a salad, they make a perfect light lunch. When fresh raspberries are out of season, frozen berries work well, but do not defrost them completely, or they will collapse; place them as directed a few minutes before serving to let them defrost. Or substitute a good-quality raspberry jam, which, in this case, is spread on the bread first, followed by the cheese. Pair with a fruit-forward white or rosé wine.

CONTORNO: Spinach and radicchio salad, plus extra berries.

$^{1}/_{3}$ cup balsamic vinegar

2 teaspoons brown sugar

Unsalted butter, at room temperature, for spreading

4 large, $^{1}/_{2}$-inch-thick slices ciabatta bread

4 ounces soft goat cheese

$^{1}/_{2}$ pint fresh raspberries

Coarsely ground black pepper

In a small, heavy saucepan, mix the balsamic vinegar and the brown sugar and cook over medium heat, stirring occasionally, until reduced by half, about 6 minutes. Set aside. You can use it warm or at room temperature.

Lightly butter the bread on both sides. Preheat a panini grill to high. Toast the bread on both sides until just golden with a tender crumb. Spread the goat cheese evenly on the bread slices. Top with as many berries as will fit. Sprinkle with pepper and drizzle with a generous amount of the balsamic reduction. Serve any extra berries on the side or pass them separately in a small bowl.

BRIOCHE AND ICE CREAM PANINI

PANINI DI BRIOCHE E GELATO serves 4

If you don't eat at least one of these when you visit Sicily, you will have missed a major highlight of your journey. Everyone there—young, old, and in between— lives on them. They are addictive. If you use your own brioche, so much the better. To eat them, hold the brioche like a regular sandwich and eat with gusto. Do not ever serve with a spoon or fork! It just wouldn't be Sicilian. Use your favorite flavor of gelato, or a mix; to me, pistachio is best, followed by vanilla, chocolate, or almond.

CONTORNO: Just serve as is.

4 individual brioches or 8 ¾-inch-thick slices brioche loaf

1 quart gelato (any flavor)

Halve each brioche almost all the way through and gently pry open like a book. For ease of assembly, slice the gelato as best you can (although scoops of gelato are fine, too). Place some gelato in each brioche "pocket" and gently push the roll sides in just to hold the panino together. If you are using sliced brioche loaf, put the gelato between 2 slices of bread. In either case, the brioche should look overstuffed with gelato! Serve immediately wrapped in parchment paper or waxed paper for ease of eating.

OVEN-ROASTED FRUIT OPEN-FACED PANINI

PANINI APERTI ALLA FRUTTA AL FORNO serves 4

In summer, this is my usual offering with a sweet dessert wine or tea, and I proudly announce how healthy it is. You can prepare the fruit several hours ahead, but be sure it is at room temperature before baking the panini.

CONTORNO: Just serve as is.

1   cup dry, big, rich red wine

2   tablespoons bitter honey, such as chestnut blossom (fior' di castagno)

1   perfectly ripe peach, pitted and cut into 1-inch dice, any juice reserved

2   large perfectly ripe plums, pitted and cut into 1-inch dice, any juice reserved

2   perfectly ripe apricots, pitted and cut into 1-inch dice, any juice reserved

4   large, ripe black or green fresh figs, stemmed, skin on, quartered

1/2 pint blueberries

4   large, 1-inch-thick slices ciabatta bread

3   tablespoons extra virgin olive oil or unsalted butter

In a small saucepan, combine the wine and honey and cook over medium heat until reduced by half, about 10 minutes. Set aside to cool.

Put the cooled wine-honey mixture into a large bowl and add the peach, plums, apricots, figs, and blueberries. Let macerate about 15 minutes.

Preheat the oven to 400°F. Toast the bread on one side on medium heat using a panini grill or an iron skillet with a 1-pound weight on the bread. Generously grease a baking pan with sides with oil or butter. Place the bread on the baking sheet, toasted sides up. Spoon the fruit and some of the fruit juices on each slice of bread. Do not soak the bread; extra juice can become a little sauce later. Bake about 15 minutes, or until the tips of the fruit are gilded, but do not let the bread dry out. Serve hot or warm. If you have leftover marinating juice or fruit, pass it separately.

CHEESE AND APRICOT PRESERVES PANINI

PANINI DI FORMAGGIO E MARMELLATA *serves 4*

In the cold of northern Italy, which abounds in magnificent cheeses, there are also many delicious fruit preserves. Apricot is my favorite, and with this smooth, nutty cheese, nothing is better. Serve with a glass of fruit-forward white wine, such as Kerner or Müller-Thurgau. (Sometimes these panini are my breakfast.)

CONTORNO: Walnut halves, Belgian endive leaves, and thinly sliced raw crimini mushrooms.

- 4 ciabatta rolls, halved lengthwise, or 8 ³/₄-inch-thick slices ciabatta bread
- 4 tablespoons unsalted butter, at room temperature
- 6 tablespoons chunky apricot preserves
- 6 ounces thinly sliced Taleggio, Montasio, or Asiago cheese

Preheat a panini grill to high. Toast the bread quickly on one cut side to mark with golden stripes. Spread butter on the toasted sides of the roll bottoms, then spread on the apricot preserves, and top with some of the cheese. Cover with the roll tops. Grill the panini on medium heat until the cheese barely begins to melt and the bread is golden. Cut each panino in half for convenient eating. Serve warm.

DRIED FRUIT AND MASCARPONE PANINI

PANINI DI FRUTTA SECCA E MASCARPONE *serves 4*

I find these panini easy to make and terrific for a no-notice lunch when friends drop by unexpectedly. Served with a few slices of high-quality prosciutto or salami, you make *la bella figura* and eat well, too.

My favorite dried fruit is figs, which are available year round and have an intense and satisfying flavor. If you must substitute the mascarpone, don't use cream cheese; it tastes too "American." Instead, try a goat cheese, a soft cheese such as La Tur (from Italy's Piedmont region), or a good French brie.

CONTORNO: Toasted nuts, such as almonds and walnuts, and thinly sliced fresh bulb fennel.

12 dried Calimyrna or Mission figs (about ¾ ounce each)

Apricot preserves, for spreading (optional)

½ pint mascarpone cheese

4 ciabatta rolls, halved lengthwise

Unsalted butter, at room temperature, for spreading (optional)

In a heavy saucepan, blanch the dried figs in rapidly boiling water over medium-high heat for about 5 minutes. Remove from the pan and dry on paper towels. Trim off the stems and cut the figs into slices about ¼ inch thick.

Preheat a panini grill to medium. Spread a thin layer of apricot preserves on the bottom halves of the rolls, if you wish, then a generous amount of mascarpone. Top with a single layer of dried figs about ¼ inch thick. Cover with the roll tops. You can lightly butter the outsides of the bread before grilling, if you like. Grill the panini until the bread is golden and warm, about 10 minutes. Cut each panino in half and serve warm.